Defiance
come out 8 mos
preg

Opposite of WK

Rose

Suspension

Helen - 20 yrs

Pam
I'm no
match
for it

Breasts
Credibility
purge
at Br

Over 40

more incidents
than Pikki
Delaney
or Kathy
Acker

making, mating
spreading a fact over
dimensions

vs.
Tom Wolfe

Career -
104

End 1 Ali

The Room Lit *by* Roses

ALSO BY CAROLE MASO

Ghost Dance

The Art Lover

The American Woman in the Chinese Hat

AVA

Aureole

Defiance

Break Every Rule

The Room Lit *by* Roses

A JOURNAL OF PREGNANCY AND BIRTH

Carole Maso

COUNTERPOINT
WASHINGTON, D.C.

LIBRARY OF CONGRESS CATALOGING-IN-PUBLICATION DATA
Maso, Carole.
The room lit by roses : a journal of pregnancy and birth / Carole Maso.
p. cm.
ISBN 1-58243-088-8 (alk. paper)
1. Maso, Carole. 2. Novelists, American—20th century—Biography. 3. Lesbian mothers—United States—Biography. 4. Pregnant women—United States—Biography. 5. Mothers and daughters. 6. Childbirth. 7. Pregnancy. I. Title.
PS3563.A786 Z47 2000
813'.54—dc21
[B] 00-038423

Quotations on pages 9, 10, 11, 19, 27, and 102 are from *The First Nine Months of Life* by Geraldine Lux Flanagan. A Touchstone Book, Simon & Schuster, 1962.

FIRST PRINTING
Jacket and text design by Amy Evans McClure
Printed in the United States of America on acid-free paper that meets the American National Standards Institute Z39–48 Standard.

COUNTERPOINT
P.O. Box 65793
Washington, D.C. 20035–5793
Counterpoint is a member of the Perseus Books Group

10 9 8 7 6 5 4 3 2 1

The Room Lit *by* Roses

FOR A LONG TIME I HAD wanted a child, but the desire, attenuated, had passed, and other feelings had taken its place. I had become so entranced by the utterly hypnotic path I found myself on, so bleary, so consumed by my work, that I had lost track of whatever else I may have once wanted. I had wandered away into a kind of otherworldly bliss, a joy like no other, and the child further and further off on some remote horizon had become a shadow—like almost everything else in my world. From those weird, windy, solitary heights from which I worked now I watched the child wave, wave, and then finally vanish. Disappeared on a beautiful, curving planet—utterly out of reach. A distant, infinitesimal music.

The Bay of Angels, a book I had just begun composing after ten years of note-taking, was to be the project for the rest of my life; I was quite certain of it—and the prospect of a life of such possibility and pleasure and challenge was more than I had ever dared ask or hope for. Over the years it had slowly grown in me—each book I had written was preparation for it. Time was passing and the urgency, as Stein said, "to write something down someday in my own handwriting" was pressing. The chance to get closer to the eternity in myself. I was ready at last. It was clear to me that in order to even attempt such an endeavor more sacrifices would have to be made. But they were well worth it—had always been worth it. The accompanying melancholy was just part of the bargain, the demands such work makes, the tolls it takes, simply part of the deal. I thought of Beckett's "sadness after song." Sadness because it was so imperfect and inadequate and fleeting, because it demanded absolutely everything. I watched the child recede.

With every major decision there is regret, for the very act involves choosing one thing over another. I have always experienced a certain sorrow when any project I am working on begins to take a shape and becomes a stable, definitive text—because it excludes the thousand books it might have been. No matter how spacious, no matter how suggestive or fluid, I cannot help but feel the death of possibility all over again—the books that now would never be. I have never felt completely reconciled to that fact. *This and not that.*

The sadness after song. I would not mind. If song it was I got to sing.

How then to account for the wave of clarity that passed through me, propelling me into an utterly charmed and charged night to retrieve that little waving figure who was mine? The child I had spent years writing about in my *Bay of Angels* notebooks. When I look back I see that she is there in one way or another in many, many guises. My writing life, as always, so much further ahead of my conscious, rational mind. How had I been so blind? There she was at the periphery of every page, waiting, begging at the edge of language, calling my name. But I did not, could not recognize her—until it was very nearly too late.

With the child revealed and the desire no longer disguised, the exact right moment with the exact right person came with strange speed—in an instant, in motion, and under a sky of enormous beauty and calm. A trillion spermatozoa and the serenity of the egg, and she is made. After one night. I was sure of it even then. Such was my improbable bravada—knowing full well the difficulty of conception after thirty-five, let alone after forty. And knowing also all that could go wrong even if by some miracle the child in a single night might materialize. Still there was not one moment of doubt or uncertainty. Doubt had passed. I was as lucid as I have ever been. I moved toward the moment embracing its strangeness, its odd gravity, filled with a mystic's faith. And the man. I think now he must have known or sensed there was something extraordinary taking place between us—as we traveled in the night backward and forward toward the child. Did this mysterious *l'étranger* from a far-off land, who uncannily had also existed in my pages for many years, somehow see in me a brilliance, illuminated as I must have been by my longing? It is a fairy tale, a story of such unlikeliness and charm. We came together without will almost, caught in the motion, without choice—and this pull, unlike anything I had felt before, this strangeness, might have been called in another time *destiny, fate.* The child just outside us, asking for the mere chance to live. Mere, indeed. Did we dare turn away from her? Did we dare ignore her pleas? In that night of ever expanding circles, heavenly bodies. The stars aligned. A primal ancient motion—the violence of creation, and then rest.

I know from Latin that *amniotic* means lamb. An odd thing. How I have called this back I do not know, but I am certain of it the way people are certain of things in dreams.

Just months ago, Helen, my companion of the last twenty years—that is my whole life—had prayed over the relics of every saint in Tuscany and Umbria for a child. We had ended finally in Assisi, first at St. Francis's Cathedral where I had wept in front of the Giottos and the Cimabues—that little piece of Paradise—and then where we had descended the dark stairs to the reliquary and witnessed at the crypt a bride and groom exchanging vows. Oh, the Italians know how to have a wedding, I remember thinking. Afterwards we made our way up the pilgrim's road to the Cathedral of St. Clare, and it is the weird thing about Assisi—or maybe it is, after all, the weird thing about me—but despite the crowds, the town seemed completely hushed, a village of silence and birds. We were caught in some incredible stillness, mystery, abyss. I do not question such things too closely. It was what I noticed. The birds sucked up in some God vortex. And Helen, struck by this holy place, whispered ferociously over the relics of the saint to me: *Pray for the baby.* What extraordinary role did Helen play in allowing the child through to the other side? And serene, recumbent Saint Clare in that most humble and sacred of places . . .

We had prayed to every saint, martyr, and of course the Virgin for this baby and now—I was only a few days late—one could only hope. Helen rose at 6 A.M. and drove through fog to the CVS pharmacy for the home pregnancy test. What does CVS stand for? I wondered. CVS, just another fin-de-siècle beacon, without meaning. I tried not to take it as a sign for something. Would the test be positive, would the test be negative? I let the question flicker in my head, savoring the last few moments before absolute certainty. I believed I knew but I had been wrong before. Holding the wand in the early morning fog, I passed it through my urine—*two stripes* and the child is found.

For luck—and from now on everything will be done for luck, whether it is eating a Peking duck or wearing a certain blue scarf or playing Bach, Beethoven, Brahms, Bruckner, Britten, Bartók—this day we go to the Poet's Walk, a place I suppose it was imagined certain romantic pastorals might be composed. A blue mountain, a white gazebo. *There is a child,* is our ode.

In an instant my own childhood floods back. That daydreaming girl, swinging on her swing, long ago. The heart rising and falling. Again and again. Buoyancy of the afternoon. If you could make one wish what would it be? I'd ask myself. One and only one.

We meet my family at the Dutchess County Sheep Show. Everyone looks different observed through the lens of the miraculous. It is news that must be kept secret for the first three months, there is no question. Too many things could go wrong. To attach language to such catastrophe were it to happen would not be possible. To imagine having to casually engage in a dialogue of vanishing, to have to accept consolation. But I am far from cautious today. Wildly ecstatic, already in mourning, I pet the head of every sheep I see. *Lamb, be with me.* Everywhere I look there is beauty and fire this October afternoon, wonder and iridescence. It feels like a celebration. *Placenta* in Latin means cake.

I have the makings of an excellent Catholic, I think, in spite of everything, because my disposition leads me to the most excessive forms of adoration. I am particularly drawn to that which does not necessarily exist.

If I could make one wish, I'd wish for this.

I can scarcely believe what lives inside me—if only for this one moment. I look out at the transfigured universe.

My heart fills the world like Magritte's rose.

Helen wants to buy tiny lamb's-wool booties, little hats, baby buntings, everything she sees—but I say we must wait, not yet. As if one could stave off heartbreak by the refusal of baby booties. The next few months will be the hardest. Still, at the center I feel an extraordinary calm. A feeling that has eluded me my whole life until now. I hold the entire body of a lamb in my arms. I pray: *Sheep may safely graze.*

15 OCTOBER

I cannot rouse myself. Cannot even imagine getting up. How to get to school? The world going on out there, I suppose. This fatigue like no other. This distance. How small the rest of the world from here. How far off. Never felt such fatigue, such silence, such peace—

Compelled as I am, pulled down an *allée*, a line of trees, a line of plain trees, *France?* Into an overwhelming calm and strangeness.

Sleep now for this insomniac.

Odd, as if one's whole life were being rocked.

18 OCTOBER

And this I think is what dying must be like. Everything small as if seen from a great distance. The fierce attachments to this world begin to loosen. I give up a little. Strangely, without even trying. Good-bye. And if this is what dying is . . . the world a tender place—I look back on it with fondness. As it disappears, losing its hold on me, I realize I have really very few regrets. In fact none come readily to mind—that I did not have more time to write, yes, but nothing else, nothing enormous. I think I must be a very lucky person that this be so. This letting go is a gorgeous thing. The ground beneath my feet gives way to something quite else. And I glimpse for a moment—for one moment it opens in me, but then passes—only intimations, but intimations nonetheless of what seems to be eternity.

Two three-hour workshops in the same day, and I am exhausted.

Reading an undergraduate paper aloud in class we come to the line, "Walter's long knife slices the duck again and again, crispy skin crinkling itself at the edge of the plate with each smooth cut."

We are here to comment on the paper. But I am beast. Like my cat, Fauve, focused on that one thing—that morsel that might drop. Cannot recall such hunger. And rarely such strange single-mindedness. Cannot pry my mind from the crispy skin. Cannot think. In the purity of this hunger zone, where I collapse, defenseless. Feed me. Cover me. Put me to sleep. I am beast. I look up at the class, speechless.

My mane grows wild and I stare. Into space forever. Lion haired. My nails grow strong and sharp. The eye searching the horizon line. Feed me, warm me, put me to bed. Shred clothing, paper. Build me a fire. Dark flame—

Small flame. Like the heart clinging. Tenacity. I pray for you. Ferocity. I am over forty. That you might hold.

I am all beauty. All beast. Something so startling. Like Rilke's panther. I am all want, hope, desire, fear.

In the book the enormity, the serenity, the perfection of the egg. The supreme solitude of the egg . . .

A shining sperm breaks through. The sperm nucleus and the egg nucleus lie side by side and their content is combined.

Large and luminous and perfectly still. Frantic motion just outside her. Perfectly round and lit from within. Shimmering. Transparent.

Creation's momentous drama: "That moment, when the two nuclei form and the now fertilized egg divides in two, is the beginning of the life of the new individual. This is zero hour of Day One."

On that plane. All altitude, velocity, the collapsing past, the future right there, next to me. He is speaking to me. I am all lucidity, and in an instant I reach out. Light bounces wildly in the cabin. The blur of voice and hand—speed, accuracy, certitude, at these heights. What were our choices? A star is slung over our heads and the earth is turning at an incredible speed, and we are both dizzy with so many things—the real world tiny, the world beneath dissolving. Maybe I am crazy. This is the moment; I am quite sure. No, maybe not. I am dying in the instant I turn away from it—and so I turn back. We are alive. Before my eyes a rose, a wing, a star. That one held note. My life a vulnerable, fragile, fleeting thing. Liquid and urgent. Stars contained in a bowl. I glitter. He lifts his hand to the light. All is movement and the movement is unspeakably beautiful. We take flight. *Maybe we could get together some other time.* I was the one who said, *tonight.* I took his hand. And we descend. Curve of the land. All that was, or is, or will ever be possible, in this one moment. Afterwards an incredible calm.

The drift of you and stars in the dark. Through the lily- or trumpet-shaped fallopian tubes, past the uterus and into the womb—you are already beautiful. Free floating. Free.

That silent drift—a lovely music.

The cells multiply, the code is passed, and she is made. When the four-day-old cell cluster arrives in the womb, it is made up of three dozen cells. Closely packed together, they are known as *morula*—from the Latin for mulberry.

My beautiful mulberry girl.

"A pale-lavender spongy surface, and on it a tiny blister surrounded by crimson. The crimson wreath is the slight wound caused by the invasion into the maternal tissues."

Oh, baby-to-be in your capsule of blood.

The cluster of follicle cells around the ovum is a beautiful radiant wreath and so it is called the *corona radiata.*

The three dozen cells of the mulberry are already differentiated. One layer will produce the nervous system, one layer the digestive, and the third the skeleton, heart, blood vessels, muscles. It nests finally, comes to rest, nourished by my blood.

Then two cells, four, six, eight. The structural code in place.

Dear creature. Dear miracle. Made in motion, under the stars. And you take your first shape. Two cells, four. Now legs. Heart.

To conception I brought the same things I bring to my writing: focus, faith, will, intuition, license, rigor, and recklessness. A position of mind that allows, within a structure of my own making, for the accidental, the unexpected, the contingent. To hold one's mind and body and spirit at exactly the right angle—ready for whatever will happen. Taking full advantage of a moment should it, no matter how fleetingly, present itself. Once again my writing has taught me how to live.

25 OCTOBER

By the twenty-first day that black dot is a retina. The foot like a fan. I cannot imagine anything more lovely. Already the whole embryo is formed. "It is the size of half a pea, fragile as jelly and almost without substance." I tremble to read this. The heart beating by the twenty-fifth day—it is a large bulge. This heart, dear God, in proportion to the size of the body, is nine times as large as the adult heart. I read now all that has already transpired without me, it seems.

Much more sensitive now to sound, to touch, taste, color, motion, light—and this makes it possible to mistake it for nausea. But it is not nausea—it's just the whole world heightened and spinning, sort of.

In fact, I feel in the perfect center of health. An incredible surge of well-being. Flushed with blood and hope.

27 OCTOBER

Snow falls in Michigan though it is not yet Halloween. It feels as if it comes from some magic and momentary world. C.D. and I near Ann Arbor to do a reading.

This bath of hormones.

Wideness of the Midwest. Wideness of my heart at this very moment. C.D. is out walking. I feel her life out there. Precious, singular. My friend in the first moments of snow. She has not brought her winter coat with her. I wrap her in my mind's wool. A new feeling about every creature that lives.

I think of all the snow I've walked through—anxious to greet the oblivion—longing for it as I always have. The blinding white. I walk to it still, now carrying a crimson wreath.

The skin does glow—the child shows through. All who see me comment on this, though they do not yet know. It is still our secret. What is luminous is something in the process of forming. The thousand stages of one's becoming. I am amorphous—even more so than usual—liquid. An enigma to myself—even more so than usual.

Floating in your fluid-filled chamber in silence. Tiny astronaut in your blue world, silent sphere. I wish I could work myself back far enough to that place so as to finally understand—but what? Understand what?

Not so much nausea as a slight queasiness mainly detectable through a feeling of bodily uncertainty, fragility, vulnerability—as if the earth I walked on were trembling.

30 OCTOBER

This slight remove. I am a beat or two outside almost everything—the commotion—one can detect it—particularly here at school—the flurry of academic life and all that means—I am a freshman advisor? *What—who signed me up?* And yet I am not part of it all, decidedly. Like some Zen goddess, I observe human frailty and foibles, all that is useless or stupid, with affection. Our English Department meetings, for instance. All the buffoons, the dour disciplinarians, the nutty professors, the crazies—all playing their parts—the earnest-to-a-fault assistant professors, the "artists." That would be Keith Waldrop and me, there at every meeting, don't ask me why, quietly staring into the absurd. Each and every meeting always of the *utmost importance.* Full of sound and fury. I don't mind. They are oddly amusing from this vantage point. I look on with a strange mercy, intimations of total, dare I say it, well-being. The poignancy of the diminishing world. I wave and smile. Harboring a secret universe inside. For once meeting the human race halfway. New feelings for all things born. And all things that will die.

Wish I could finish up my small book on Frida Kahlo. Even though I am nearly done, it still requires keeping my eyes open and that is not really possible to do.

The greatest risk at this point for a woman my age is miscarriage. I worry it in some part of my brain all night and all day.

Only Helen to confide in. She says, "You are a tough old bird. Try and relax."

Before I knew I was pregnant, on the way to the New York Film Festival, happy as I had ever been, writing a piece in my little *Bay of Angels* notebook. Off to see the new Antonioni film—a ticket in the second row, where I like it best. Afterwards, part of the way home, I realized I had lost my notebook. What was most interesting was that for once I did not panic. I was not filled with the usual doom. What is this peace? I remember wondering. This unusual grace? I knew when I went back it would be there, and it was. I should have known something had radically changed in me.

What grows in me. More than simply the child. What continues to grow.

The depths of this emotion. The bottom continually falling out.

Until it scarcely seems possible. I am voracious, ravenous, lustful, exhausted—everything heightened, enlarged—not to mention the breasts.

As if being under a spell, more of a trance even, than my usual one.

Close your eyes. The recurring refrain these days.

Students come for meetings and I talk to them with my head on my desk. In the M.F.A. program here anything goes, and they assume it is just another one of those things. I lift my head slightly. How is your thesis going?

It is the longest autumn I can remember. The leaves refuse to fall. They've turned extraordinary colors—do I see them accurately? I wonder. In this heightened season. Tenacious—refusing to drop. Use these trees as your example, little one.

I haul huge pumpkins around with my parents at the Grieg Farm. Lifting, I'm told, is no problem. Still, why do I risk it? The desire not to turn into a neurotic invalid, I guess. Lifting huge pumpkins! I immediately regret it. Somewhere there must be still some ambivalence. This holding on and letting go at the same time.

What I have always wanted when I think of some future world without my mother and father in it. What I always imagined might console. To have a little piece of them. To replace. To populate. A crazy, primitive notion, really. In the face of any great loss—to somehow fill up the world. To love through and beyond it, into this.

This.

Day thirty-three is a busy day, or so they say. The hand sections begin to show the outlines of fingers, the nose and upper jaw begin to form. The eyes are dark for the first time because pigment has just formed in the retina. The brain on this day is one-fourth larger than it was two days earlier. Baby, I'm amazed.

I have never felt compelled to keep a journal. On occasion I have with all good intentions attempted to record the flow of my life—only after a few weeks to leave it behind. Why? Depletion, I suppose, in part. Far too many hours were spent composing fiction—every waking hour, it seemed, every sleeping hour. I couldn't bear the thought of any more words. A journal, while an intriguing notion to me, was only that in the end, and kept very sporadically at best. Making fictive structures so much of the time, journal writing for me simply lacked a certain edge I had come to expect from composition. A journal lacked the tautness. I must say the idea of keeping an ongoing record of *my life* exhausted me, bored me, even appalled me a little. I could never keep my enthusiasm for the thing going. I never imagined words as a means to knowing how I felt—or to understanding something. And so there was no question of it serving any therapeutic ends, God knows. Quite the opposite, I feel suspicious of that earnest attempt at explanation—it always seems oddly reductive. I can't make language do those things.

But it is different with this. The perception of time, ordinarily fuzzy for me—I worked vaguely by seasons or semesters—had in an instant changed. I moved out of the blur of my life and was placed into the crucible of time. Suddenly I was counting—week four, week five—and noticing the daily changes.

Meanwhile there were all sorts of little books to keep me company—what was happening exactly, and how I was feeling probably and was going to feel. I've never felt so—well—so narrated, so attended to, accompanied. Falling into chronology. The consolation of it. And wanting to chronicle it, hold it all, keep it somehow. How strange to feel the explicit workings of time on the psyche and on the body. The dramatic workings of time: to be inside it—intimate with it like never before. To be able to feel its accomplishments.

This will all disappear, will fall eventually back into abstraction, or remain forever in my heart unarticulated and then, after a while, lost altogether. This book is a chalice. And my body now is a chalice—holding the most sacred, most precious . . . Keep this. Memorize this. Hold this time close, regardless of the outcome. I don't want to lose this. For I have never felt this way before and will never feel this way again.

And at once, the utter timelessness of the experience. I feel as if I am floating in some sort of blue suspension. I look out the window. Another train trip from New York to Providence. Providence to New York.

The upper curvature of the uterus. Nesting there.

Extreme delight these days in the body and all the body can do.

The upper curvature of the uterus. I imagine I see that shape now wherever I turn.

"She moved in circles and those circles moved."

—*Theodore Roethke*

To simply record, without embellishment, without conscious intervention or formalization, as much as is possible. Free for once of fiction's incredible demands.

To be freed for once of the burden and joy of making artful shapes. To just write—as if, after all these years, one could.

How to describe these feelings as they now come on—they resist description. A humbling experience—yet again—what refuses to pass into "writing."

The child I had written of again and again. More and more in the last few years. Let her enter these pages now unadorned.

Without the press or need for invention. To not invent a single thing. To have this be enough. More than enough. Of course. To live and write purely, in naiveté with you. A whole other way of being on the page.

Utterly mysterious, miraculous, and simultaneously mundane —*this world.*

I'd like in a spare minute to re-read Tarkovsky's *Sculpting in Time.* The hardest thing about teaching and directing some days is the lack of a private life—the ability to read whatever I like. And in a way to be who I really am.

All that escapes the page, alas. As usual. Do your best.

The arms as long as exclamation points(!!) have hands with fingers and thumbs. The ears take shape. They form in unison as do the hands and the feet. The legs have knees and ankles and toes. "The time schedule for the formation of the body is generally so consistent that it has been possible to set down the agenda of development for each day of the first forty-eight days of life."

And so it is possible to say, when asked what you have been doing—made two human feet today.

Do not pretend, Carole, that you are not frightened.

That a human being's birth dooms it to death is a truth impossible to escape.

My life now a double secret. My life a double mystery. A silence like no other. A silence magnified.

The pure violence of nature. The godlessness of it—pure force, the drive to live—the desire to take shape—anything to be made, to stay. I feel it running riot in my body. It is part of the enormous exhaustion.

An odd state. Presence and absence. Between sleep and waking. Speech and speechlessness. The God and the not God. The celebration of his absence. The inkling of his presence.

I feel astounded today by my own beauty, which is not an ordinary beauty but something else. Astounded in the end by my own resourcefulness.

I've got to say I'm really quite pleased with myself. I am no longer someone I entirely recognize. A kind of wayward halo—least likely to become an angel or a chalice—and yet . . .

To be myself and yet to be so much greater than myself.

Last summer after our trip to Italy, a few days back home, and there was a dead rabbit on the garden path. I remember it precisely. Back in the old days wasn't it when the rabbit died that one was pregnant? The so-called rabbit test. I took it as a sign. Immediately called Helen at work. Its dead bunny fur blowing in the wind. The next day it was completely gone, disappeared, eaten by animals or birds.

It's a sign, I said. I swear to you. It won't be long now, I tell her.

Carole, you are crazy.

2 NOVEMBER, ALL SOULS DAY

Pray the baby holds.

Stay. Be mine.

MONDAY, 3 NOVEMBER—EIGHT WEEKS

A drop of blood. Not even a drop of blood but a pinkish color on the toilet paper. This happening during the break in the graduate workshop. I considered canceling the rest of class so I could sit at home and worry in peace but decided LaDawn and Mary-Kim, two of my students who are mothers, will protect me.

Read brand-new work from *The Bay of Angels* to a very nice group of psychoanalysts last night. A long question-and-answer session afterward. Felt the enormity of the book. I need uninterrupted time. I need more than all the time in the world in order to pull it off. A pinkish stain on the tissue.

I have waited until the last moment to conceive a child. Filled with ambivalence. What about the book? How badly I need to write this one. Different than the others—though of course there was urgency with each project. Do I let these feelings in now as protection against the drop of blood? Should things not work out.

To hold the two simultaneously. To not deny either. Writing has taught me as much. An endeavor of utter discipline and utter playfulness. Rigor and recklessness. To control and to relinquish control.

Want. Dread. Resignation. Extraordinary hope.

I worry about the book I have waited so long to write, prepared my whole life to write. Have I subverted myself? And does this bring on the pinkish stain? Ten years of note-taking. My first extended break from teaching in seven years coming up next year. What have I done?

How to describe the blur of being pregnant? The frame holds a moment longer than it should, and I am left behind a fraction of a beat, always a fraction of a beat. But it accumulates—accretion of the beats—lagging slightly behind—until suddenly I am out of the loop, and I can't imagine the way back—the way of catching up anymore.

For years I believed I would have a child. And then for years I believed I would not.

And now this. I am close. Miracle, Aishah says. Gift from God. I know when she says it, in that voice of hers, that she is right.

Aishah says it is a miracle and also the most natural thing in the world. I tell her I live in dread of miscarriage. Don't act like such a white person, she says. Relax.

Why does it surprise me so? I have been writing her for years now. Conjuring her. Loving her. This little one.

This horizon of child.

Soon the skeleton, still cartilage, will be replaced by bone. I have been very busy today making bones, I say when Helen calls.

Fifteen

How you kept checking your panties, leaving Algebra II every twenty minutes or so, hoping, hoping, looking for a trace of blood, one spot, a pinkish tint. You had, you were sure, detected the hint of a menstrual cramp, certainly you had, there was no mistaking—and you were elated. You pressed your belly in, you prayed. You walked home in such a way as to pass the maximum number of red street signs, so as to suggest something to your body. You sang every song in order on the Rolling Stones'

Let It Bleed album. You played it over and over. You bargained shamelessly. Promised you would change everything about your life if only, if only—this once. You jogged in place. Lifted weights during fencing practice, and hit the red heart on your opponent's jacket with great accuracy. You were all focus, all will. Another chance. At home you kept closing closet drawers—hangers frightened you, what in a few days you might be capable of. You took scalding hot baths, said to bring on menstruation—you could no longer bear the suspense. Never in your young life had you felt such dread. The next day in Home Ec while making the improbable Welsh rarebit you felt a twinge—you were sure. And you were getting that headachy feeling you always got. But nothing more. It was winter and you thought if you saw a red bird eating a berry in a tree—you thought. Spicy foods, standing on your head, praying to the Virgin, shoveling snow . . .

Forty

You check your panties every half hour or so. You are not really late yet, but you are almost late, meaning you are right on time. You are almost always early and so in your mind you think: I am already quite late. And your excitement rises. You discount the stress you've been under lately and its role on the body's course. You reason, when in the last, oh, say twenty years have you not been under great stress? Good point. You count and recount the days on the calendar. You've got absolutely no menstrual cramps of any kind, and that in itself is a kind of miracle. By now you are usually doubled over in pain. Your breasts, which you check, stripping to the waist even during breaks in your writing workshop, seem to be swelling, my God, in fact they have never been so engorged—the first sign, is it not, of something nesting inside you? When did this desire for a child sharpen? You're not really sure it has. But it is not so much about the child maybe—it's simply the challenge now, the wanting to succeed at this thing—it's odd, you're the first to admit. You try to eliminate any ambivalence from your mind, knowing full well that this could throw off the whole project. You convince yourself you are nauseous and dizzy, and you're sure. But it passes. It passes so quickly that you can't be sure now you haven't invented it. You are disheartened. You pray, bargain, beg, if only this, you would become a different person. Motherly, in fact. Maternal. And at this moment you believe yourself—a good sign. You would, you think, do anything. You've got a desire for chocolate, which is an unusual desire for you. You check your panties in between meetings with students. You pray there is no stain, no blood. When the red dog passes you avert your eyes. You walk in such a way as to avoid the red signs. You decide to walk all the way home from Columbia University—a long walk—and on the way back you stop in at any number of houses of worship, as they are called—all faiths. You kneel at the holiest place in each. You feel like a pulsing, open secret. You are full of grace. When you arrive downtown and walk into your apartment the room is lit by roses.

How many times have I kissed the feet of the Virgin?

Back on that plane where, over the ocean, the stranger appeared in the night. Handing me a little note.

The silly things people say to one another: *You are exactly my type.* Or, *I changed my seat to be near you. Don't move. Stay just like that.* So I might memorize this moment.

Once many years ago, I met a Hungarian girl of about sixteen on a plane flying back from I cannot remember where, and I thought to myself, she is my daughter. It was the strangest sensation. I remember her exactly.

Somewhere between darkness and light. The moon on the wing. High up, close to heaven.

"An experienced seductress."

The press of water in the dark. A delectable darkness. Where the ocean opens up into a kind of infinity. And the sky.

An ocean in the window. I recall the vastness. He took my hand.

"Vintage Carole Maso," Helen says, after the shock wears off.

I carry the lines of her palms and the lines of her feet—unique to her, hers alone, in my body.

On day forty-four, twenty milk teeth are embedded in the gum ridges

I return to Blistein House, where the Creative Writing Program resides. In the past two years five baby girls have been born here.

After the initial shock Helen, who has always risen to every occasion, rises again. Helen, who has wanted this in many ways more than I have. In that kind of direct way of wanting.

We'll be a family: a baby, two cats.

We'll make it up as we go along. As we always have, I think to myself.

Deeply suspicious of convention as I have always been. Of what most people will take for granted.

In the air I told him I was writing a book about a professor who murders her students and he thinks I am a trashy novelist and I like the idea of that a great deal—free of the burden of seriousness.

I have written for the past few years again and again of children and sometimes it seems of this very child. The way the writing has worked as charm. Calling forth the child, inventing it. The word made flesh. In the perfection of the love and the faith—the writer's faith, strange talisman, protection, guide. This amazing, unlikely life of mine.

Heartbeat cling.

Now it begins: *pain au chocolat!* I cry out to Helen in the next room.

She sends pears to me in Providence. Always our lucky, our most precious fruit. They always feel like a celebration to me. A gift of pears arrives. Everything will be all right.

5 NOVEMBER

In the fallen leaves I see all the miscarried children.

Heartbeat cling.

And Chloe, what does Chloe mean? Helen thumbing through the baby name book. Too early for me to be thinking of such things. I make up a list:

take the megavitamins
no hot baths
no lifting
no caffeine

Tiny heartbeat cling.

I am like the cat who keeps turning and turning in circles trying to get comfortable. Trying to find comfort. The comfortable spot. I am like the cat. Asleep eighteen hours a day.

How Helen prayed through every village, to every saint for the child.

The grand finale in Assisi. *Maybe we should name her Chiara.*

On her knees in the modest chapel of Santa Chiara. She turning and mouthing the words in the silence: *Pray for the child.*

"The forty-day-old human is so small it would fit into a walnut. It weighs less than a book of paper matches."

Somehow, miraculously, the desire for alcohol has completely left me. And so I am not even tempted. Mercifully. And my usual desire for oblivion? The sleep of the dead that I sleep now helps that. A sleep I have never before experienced. I follow it like an addict now down into blackness.

Another miracle is the lack of nausea. Just a very, very mild queasiness that passes. Though in the back of my mind somewhere this troubles me. I think I read somewhere once that the lack of nausea is not always such a good sign. I avoid finding out the miscarriage statistics. Over forty. I don't think I would advise anyone to wait this long.

I resent the distraction of having to have a job now. Helen: *Don't be a prima donna.* I cry myself to sleep.

Another fight: *You should be able to write* and *have a job. Everyone works!* I call this the little philistine in her ear. It's her therapist speaking.

And I'd like to burrow deep into the ground with her and wait this out, hibernate, quietly, without any distraction—that is how mesmerizing this is. How beautiful it is—the calm, the dark. We could paste a few stars on the top if she'd like. I could tell stories of the sun.

I have never even come close to this much happiness. What is going on?

I love them for saying nothing, nothing will, nothing can

go wrong. My grand dames, my guides: Aishah, C.D., Rikki, Bunny, extraordinary godmothers whispering *not too old.*

The few I have told.

Angela Carter was forty-five after all, Rikki offers.

9 NOVEMBER—WEEK SEVEN

This white room of all possibility, all that ever was and ever shall ever be, which I inhabit now. Days of grace.

Practicing in the gloom my Czerny and Chamanade. Another lesson on Friday. A girl at the piano. Why does it come back now?

I see it as the final blow to men—that they can't bear children. Excluded in the end. And that nasty bit about never even being certain you have really fathered anyone.

Easier somehow all of a sudden to understand their melancholy, their rage, their insecurity. Yes, maybe.

Have I subverted myself after all in typical feminine fashion and at the most crucial and last moment? I almost got away.

These thoughts from a zone of the brain far off and yet from time to time so alarmingly close.

15 NOVEMBER

The pressure to conform is enormous. In ordinary and not-so-ordinary ways. I have pressed back against it my whole life: the pressure to make books that look like other books, to write more legibly, to give up what is mine, and quietly.

This child is freedom even now. Detached from its cumbersome accouterments: husband, siblings, minivan. Its blandness, its arrogant directives. All that smug heterosexual clubbiness—its pleased-as-punch self-congratulation. This child was created outside the usual constraints and enclosures, without the usual prescriptions, hierarchies, sentences leveled on her head.

I pray, should she come to be, that she will not hate me for it.

Drank a hot chocolate this morning before class and about an hour later while listening to final projects felt a *very, very* strange sensation inside—a kind of heaving or turning or sloughing away, and tears ran down my face. Luckily we sat in darkness in the Russell Lab's black box theater . . . How many times in the last three months have I lost this baby?

Frida Kahlo motions at the very end of her life for the wet nurse as she falls back at the end into infancy or death. Having returned to the women. That zone of comfort and peace where she is gluttonous in her desiring toward—what?

Circles within circles
swollen
engorged
targeted
to hold your mouth just so—
suckling one.

Working on my little Frida book, or trying to. Another strange project—part biography, part autobiography, part fiction, part poetry. A dialogue of sorts between Frida and me, I suppose. Thinking all week about her desire for children. And her ambivalence. It's getting closer, I think.

My students comment on how otherworldly I am looking these days. And how quiet I seem.

Votive: Child.
Because I wanted you with all my blood, but it was not to be.

In a 1930 drawing of herself and Rivera, she drew and then erased a baby Diego seen as if by X-ray vision inside her stomach: the infant's head is up, his feet are down.

Three more times she will try to have a child.

Frida had all kinds of dolls: old fashioned ones, cheap Mexican dolls made of rags or of papier-mâché. Chinese dolls are propped on a shelf near her pillow. Beside her bed is an empty doll bed where she once kept a favored doll, and three little dolls are enclosed with Rivera's baptism dress in a vitrine in her bedroom. One that she treasured, a boy doll that had been given to her beau Alejandro probably shortly after her accident, when she was hospitalized.

The earth is a grave and the earth is a garden. Poor child, rest there, poor child, play there forever. The earth holds his tiny hands, his eyes, his little genitals. Rest.

Its birth certificate filled out in elegant scroll: *His mother was Frida Kahlo.*

sorrow: child

Her journal, 1944:

My painting carries within it the message of pain . . . Painting completed my life. I lost three children . . . Paintings substituted for all of this. I believe that work is the best thing.

The cupped butterfly, painted black.

The city and bay are overwhelming. What is especially fantastic is Chinatown. The Chinese are immensely pleasant and never in my life have I seen such beautiful children as the Chinese ones. Yes, they are really extraordinary. I would love to steal one so that you could see for yourself.

The central Frida is armless

come to me

the useless umbilicus

I sell everything for nothing . . . I do not believe in illusion . . . the great vacillator. Nothing has a name. I do not look at forms . . . drowned spiders. Lives in alcohol. Children are the days and here is where I end.

The mute blue testimony. Dark afternoon that never ends. She sits at the end of the bed smoking, utterly alone. Beside her a grinning doll—together on a child's bed. Misery without end.

The dead baby, all dressed up and nowhere to go. The soles of his feet facing us—the milky eyes, the dribble of blood, Christ flagellated on his pillow—poor tiny loser, impossible, the never-to-be, poor thing. Holding a last gladiola—most funereal thing. Dressed up for Paradise.

She watched other people dance . . .

The only thing I bought here were two old-fashioned dolls, very beautiful ones. One is blonde with blue eyes, the most wonderful eyes you can imagine. She is dressed as a bride . . . Both are lovely, even with their heads a little bit loose. Perhaps that is what gives them so much tenderness and charm. For years I wanted to have a doll like that, because someone broke one that I had when I was a child, and I couldn't find it again. So I am very happy having two now. I have a little bed in Mexico, which will be marvelous for the bigger one. Think of two nice Hungarian names to baptize them.

Accident: 10 Our Father's, 10 Hail Mary's, 3 Glory Be's.

The lacerated Mexican saint
she watched other people's children. Because it was not
to be.
Pray for us sinners.
The useless petitions

3 Not to Be's
black umbilicus

paint:
an umbilical chord emerges from a placenta—the large red vein. Good-bye.

18 NOVEMBER—WEEK TEN

Finally my first visit to the doctor. Lisa Rehrer, the one we had chosen, has been sick, and so we had to reschedule a few times. She's nice, about my age. She wondered just how many babies I might be carrying as we got ready for the sonogram. Not funny. It seems that after forty the eggs start hurling themselves out two, three at a time sometimes—and so there is the possibility of more than one baby. No, not funny in the least. I feel I am ready for about anything—but not twins, let alone triplets. Good God! Mercifully I never took fertility drugs. That's one hopeful thing.

It is confirmed, one very great baby is in there! I can't describe the feeling. To see, to hear it. No words come close. The elevator on the way down from the doctor's office gets stuck and so all tears of joy must be postponed. Helen's gone ahead to get the car. It is me and a man who speaks only—it's not Spanish, so it must be Portuguese—and I am suddenly very, very panicky and claustrophobic. I am my own nest of Russian dolls in this box. These rooms within rooms making me dizzy. But it is the man who actually looks woozy. Are you sick, I ask him, pausing between my frantic attempts to reach someone on the elevator telephone. He indicates his head. *Help!* I feel like Lucy Ricardo.

Days have passed without a single word written here. I have been stunned into speechlessness. For once, no words come. Saw the little being and it has a heart beat, the baby on a TV screen. Alive there. Most extraordinary sight. Swimming. Doing little somersaults. I study the picture books now obsessively.

You fit into a goose egg now.

Songs without words.

You weigh only an ounce. But by the end of the third month you will be able to kick your legs, turn your feet, curl and fan your toes, bend your wrist, turn your head, squint, frown, open your mouth, pout.

Nothing but babies everywhere I look. These babies seek me out, speak to me. Their tiny hands, the dark *O* of their mouths —that small intake of sweet air. Stars in their hands, sparkly eyes. The chubby feet. Everywhere I turn. I try not to see this yet—or have my heart so full. Still . . .

Day after day of weeping now. This lucky, lucky life.

Do a little fan dance for me when you can.

I am grateful to have Gale, my assistant director. Teaching two classes and directing the program while I can hardly keep my eyes open would not be remotely possible without him. He does not know the news yet—I am waiting until after the amniocentesis—but still he instinctively comes to my rescue; he is always there by my side, helping with the next, and then the next, crisis. I realize I will be pregnant the entire school year.

The back and forth from Providence to New York all exhausting. Trying to read student papers on the train as much as possible. I keep drifting off. Revery of the very late fall—one of my favorite seasons. A beautiful, desolate time.

I am a good teacher because I refuse to condescend to my students, and because I listen to them and respect the work they are doing, and the terms they have set for it. I do not prejudge it. And I do not have preconceptions. In fact this is what keeps me interested in student work. I do not ask them questions to which I already know the answers. I do not want to make them over in my own image. I cannot bear the pathetic ego most writing teachers routinely assert. I only ask my students questions, and this often exasperates them, but there is no other way I can teach in good conscience. I am not a tyrant, I am not a bully, I am always kind. In an uncharacteristic moment of dismay once I told an undergraduate class that I was not going to spend more time critiquing their papers than they spent writing them. I will not be taken advantage of. I give them a lot of room in which to work. Am I too lenient? Am I too disengaged? I think not. I am not a taskmaster. Only when I sit down to write myself am I completely relentless: *you can do better than this.* But not with my students. If they do not become writers it is really quite all right with me. I cannot give them the need to write if they do not have it. Some of my Brown graduate students are so good that I consider it my job mainly to stay out of their way. I like teaching but am drained by the part of the brain it uses up. It is the same part required to write. It is, I assume, the same part it takes to raise a child creatively. If I had nine lives, teaching is what I would do with one of them. As it is I have only one.

Dreamt last night I was a belly dancer. On a table at The Magic Carpet.

In the twelfth week motion becomes specialized and graceful.

29 NOVEMBER

I am on my way to California. It is Helen's birthday. For once she got to choose her own birthday presents because I just couldn't traipse around town the way I ordinarily like to—I am just too sleepy. I didn't even wrap them this year. She's gotten me one of those suitcases you pull along, because she doesn't want me lifting anything. I do not have a phone in Providence, and she insists I get a cell phone, which she gives me with the suitcase. *What if there is an emergency?* I smile. My Buddha spirit is beginning to wear on her nerves: there will be no emergencies, I say serenely.

Babies in the air. Little diapered babies at 35,000 feet running down the aisles. Babies on those little collapsible changing tables. Babies in every lap. Beautiful, beautiful, beautiful, beautiful.

Today is Helen's birthday. I took her to the restaurant Provence for lunch before I got on the plane.

But my real gift to her of course: a baby in the air.

We are flying as the finishing touches are applied. The nail beds form on the fingertips. The eyes move toward the bridge of the nose. The eyelids close over the eyes by the ninth week and temporarily seal them like a kitten's. They will remain closed now until the sixth month. You travel in darkness for now, little one. I'm right here.

Imagined one. Prepared-for one. Loved so thoroughly in advance.

30 NOVEMBER, THE FRENCH HOTEL, BERKELEY, CALIFORNIA

Flung across time zones, gluttonous for more hours, I sleep the sleep of the dead all day, all night it seems, wake only to do my readings.

Days of rain. The Californians do not approve of rain. I'd forgotten. It's very beautiful here. I fall back to sleep.

Someone says the writer Kathy Acker is dead, and I push through fog toward the terrible news. I must be dreaming.

She has closed her eyes. They will remain closed to the sixth month. The vocal cords are complete, but in the absence of air they cannot produce sound.

That I should have been able, in this state, to protect Kathy Acker, drawn her into this bubble. That I could not do this, or any other thing—a sorrow, a reminder.

Extravagance of the fruits and flowers here!

The true test: to be in Berkeley and not drink even one cup of coffee. The most delicious coffee in the country. No latte, no leche, no capuccino, no mocha, not short, not tall, not dry, not wet . . . A strange torture.

Attractions of every sort considerably heightened in this condition. All is intensity. Extremity. The word shudder comes to mind.

The lushness and lusciousness of everything.

Read at Saint Mary's for Brenda Hillman. A delicious meal at Chez Panisse with a very fun bunch of people afterwards. Two pregnant women at our table. What a giddy, weird joy.

E. M. Ciorin:

> Children scare me. Their eyes carry too many promises of unhappiness. Why do they want to grow up? Children, like madmen, are graced with innate genius, soon lost in the void of lucidity.

Does he sentimentalize and therefore condescend to both children and madmen?

My book *Aureole* just out in paperback. When I read out loud now without a microphone I can't get enough breath in my lungs. The effect is a particularly unfortunate one, especially with this book, overheated, hothouse flower that it is.

One can only laugh.

The insistence of the heart, even through the whoosh of water, magnified on a little public address system in the doctor's office. I'm beginning to gain weight now and am already enjoying the heft.

That time—a period of several months—when every man who neared me felt that pull, that tone, that hum. The zone of fertility, the buzz of readiness, the surge of absolute ripeness. The ancient desire to replicate propels them toward me—a little bewildered, they can't stay away. I had the pick of the lot. Last summer and fall. The demands of an attraction they willingly and sometimes unwillingly found themselves caught up in. That smell, that touch, they were irresistibly drawn to—hovering near my body. I understand it now. The mating signals activated in me. And the men wild—they don't know why. I am not young anymore and have not had quite this kind of power over men in some time. They might have chosen younger, more promising specimens. If there had been a choice. But there is none.

I walk in a delirium laughing and crying. My graduate students are suspicious for I have suddenly stopped drinking altogether. It hasn't been so hard, though I did regret not being able to keep up with Harry Mathews, who was here recently for a week. An extraordinary man and one of the great joyful drinkers.

Already I have had moments of genuine mourning for my old life. Will I ever get it back again? I feel the immensity, the gravity of this even now.

My sister Cathy guesses immediately when I tell her I have something important to tell her. She is ecstatic. I think all women with children are somehow pleased when someone else joins their ranks. Company of sorts—this island of motherhood. The deep isolation of it on one level. I feel it already. Or is it just my natural predilection?

I'm eating bread with lavender honey. A hot chocolate. I'm petting a gray poodle. Eating new potatoes out of a glass bowl. Hoping.

I'm dreaming of France again.

In *The American Woman in the Chinese Hat,* I tried to write a novel that appeared desultory, like a memoir or notebook, a day book, a chronicle of a life as it unfolded. How difficult that was—to artfully make events seem random, senseless. To unmake while I was making. This kind of writing is such a new experience for me. Just allowing thoughts to occur, with a kind of coherence and randomness, without a concern for shapeliness of any kind. A weird feeling—like I should be doing something more here. All my tentacles on end. Hard to relax. To simply allow—it is something I am not at all practiced in. Oh, now I have a thought about—*my kangaroo pouch*—Well, OK, write it down!

A dream in which the entire animal kingdom paraded out displaying the various ways they carry their young.

Why, I also wonder, do I find myself protecting my privacy far more in this journal than in my fictions? I create a slightly pristine version of myself here. I need to consider the ordinary assumptions again about fiction and nonfiction. This interests me, having never written like this before.

A certain reserve. Protectiveness already. Becoming a mother.

I can begin to understand surrogate motherhood. So far at any rate. So much serenity. As if there had been a visitation by angels.

I wait for the quickening. That first flutter within. Feel part of some ancient process—women whispering, "It's the quickening. She's got the quickening." I believe I have already felt the baby move, though the books say probably no. I feel exactly like a pioneer woman for some reason.

This flying inside one's own body. The women are whispering.

15 DECEMBER—FOURTEEN WEEKS

Time for a small celebration! I have passed the first trimester without a hitch!

At Thanksgiving my mother wishing out loud for another grandchild. How can she love babies so much? I have got to tell them soon. Louis and Louise are here with us this year. They just moved nearby. I couldn't be happier about it.

A strange dream last night. The message: "Go to sleep like the flowers." Something elegiac about it.

I have finally told my parents. The first trimester up. Thanksgiving come and gone. I had wanted to tell them in person but have not been able to get home. And there seems no more delaying it. My sister Cathy has known for some time and can scarcely contain herself. I call them on the phone from my office, filled with both excitement and trepidation. Mom is delighted, if a little incredulous. Poor Dad, gasping like a ghost.

Of course my mother would have been happy even if I had stolen a baby from the Kmart, so desperate was she always that I have one. But this! She couldn't be more thrilled, though she has to be a little tempered for my father, who is having a harder time integrating the news. My mother says he hasn't spoken for days. It is not convention, but it is something, something that is troubling him.

My friend Mirielle, when thinking of adopting a half-white, half-black baby from the South. Her mother: They throw babies like that away in the garbage and you want to adopt one! Now of course she is madly in love with the child.

Stretched out she might fit on a thumbnail now. I like to think of her stretched out and floating in there on a little raft perhaps.

As Christmas nears. My favorite season. A father's fear. A mother's delight. I am their child. First born.

Nothing to dispel the strangeness that we were seven people in one house late at night, dreaming our dreams. My family.

At twelve weeks she turns away from anything that touches her. Avoids rather than seeks. Her eyes are closed. She floats.

Ten years ago in the midst of a profound depression/breakdown. When I surface at last, after much, much suffering, why is the "solution" always children?

18 DECEMBER

Why shouldn't the old models, which are working with less and less success, be challenged—the world reimagined? Heterosexual privilege and power—and all its attendant rigmarole. Such a system, if it were to be taken seriously, would have precluded me from having a child. Luckily I have never taken it even the least bit seriously.

But I have been outside of everything from the beginning—except the system of love. My mother's love and care for all those years, my father's mildness and iconoclasm, have allowed me the audacity, the courage to do what I must. But I resent, I do, that it should have to take what seems like so much more than even the ordinary courage just to be happy. Just to live. Things most take for granted. Still I am grateful for the confidence to be flexible, to do what I must, without inordinate anger or fear.

The future for you, but not only for you.

Stamped on the street some years ago before Gay Pride Weekend: *Every Kiss a Revolution.*

The jig, I'm afraid, is increasingly closer to being up. As soon as cloning is perfected. A sheep now made from two eggs . . . Dolly.

Ate for lunch today many turkey sandwiches.

When I was little my mother was always pregnant. No one ever explained to me how this happened, and my assumption of course was that it was all some cruel and useless roulette: God would decide and that was that. The question was how to hide from Him, how to make yourself invisible, inconspicuous. All women victims of His Whims. My mother always seemed to me exhausted, burdened. All the responsibility fell to her. It was a terrible thing. I felt for her a great deal.

When I was little, and God was big.

Our lake life. Bliss in every way. Except—something nags, gnaws—even in my preconsciousness, when I was very, very young. Why are there always so many babies? We live— minuscule, laughable creatures on that bobbing platform in water at the mercy of that whimsical, practical-joking God—women do, girls do, even here in Paradise, in bright light, next to shining water. I am always braced for the news: we are having another baby.

I decided early on through sheer will, through presence of mind, sheer attentiveness, whatever it might take, that I would not allow this to happen to me. I remember as a little girl repeating it in my room over and over and over. Casting spells to keep Him away. I would ask Mary when the time came to intercede on my behalf. So enormous a hindrance to living one's life, children seemed to me. I could not have been more than eight years old at the time.

And when I got my first period at twelve years old, one of the first things my mother said to me was, now you can have a baby. I sat at the dark keyboard practicing my scales, and wept.

And a few years later when she comes into my room and asks whether I would mind sharing my room with a new baby. *Yes,* I say, I would mind. The child never arrives. I do not ask why.

A cautionary tale I took to heart.

I think of my mother often these days. That she did not have a mother to talk with, to console her, to reassure her as she went through her pregnancies. And pregnancy of course brings up one's own mother hundreds of times.

No feminine support of any sort for her back then. I feel her loss more keenly now than ever before. A loss now over fifty years old.

Poverty. A mortally ill mother. Other things, unmentioned. *The saddest of all childhoods.*

I tell them on the way to the concert that in this child I will have a part of them always. I picture their deaths, the way I did obsessively when I was little. This makes me weep uncontrollably as we drive through the darkness and the cold. I am a child again. Completely vulnerable. I have always loved them too much. My father is beginning to speak again. He has found the way to voice his concerns: what about money? What about my writing? What about my health? Will it be dangerous?

The most difficult things about having a baby at my age are, first, conceiving at all; second, keeping the child, that is, not miscarrying in the first trimester; and third, getting past the possibility of birth defects. All those old eggs, etc. All that bad environment on the body. All the compromised earth one has taken in having lived this long. Oh, God. The third is the only real worry now.

And money? It comes, it goes, there is nothing really that can be done about it. At least I have a so-called real job. My writing? I pretend I am not worried about it. It will make my writing better, I say, having no real idea what I am talking about.

Apparently if I can make it through the first trimester and the amniocentesis, then I am as home free as anyone ever is in this. Some risk, but not undo. He is concerned about me. I am his daughter. His firstborn. Of course.

Exhilarating to finally be this near to having a child on my own terms. To have made the whole thing up.

The Lord is with thee . . . Never have I understood these words as I understand them now. Certainly someone, certainly someone or something is with me. The light is with me—at least that.

That I had walked at 4 A.M., most terrible hour of the day, of the night, in utter fear and dread, in utter sorrow, scarcely breathing, to kiss my dead friend good-bye, and that now I walk through that exact door again in such elation and hope, and some fear also. It does not seem possible, not in one lifetime. West Twelfth Street. Saint Vincent's Hospital.

That same threshold.

No visitor's passes needed to visit the dead. They direct me solemnly an alternate way. I still remember.

A journal is interesting in that it records the instants of life as they pass. And an instant of thought and of writing as it takes shape, the words as they form. Fragile, evolving, and in motion. Continuous and discontinuous. Stated, erased, restated. Not made or shaped as fiction for the most part is. Not one invented thing. As much as is possible.

An honoring of the contingent, the mark on the page—without embellishment, without revision or amendment.

The revolving doors were locked at 4 A.M. Michael and I had breakfast together afterwards. Patrick later in the hallway, because I went back, because I could not leave yet. *Where is Gary?*

He's been taken to be cremated, I think.

I am losing a certain edge. What a relief to be a little free of myself. A break from the intensity. This bovine happiness. I think about trying to complete Frida but it seems far away—and I'm really too sleepy. I am only grateful that I finished every single aspect of *Defiance* before this all began. It would not have been possible to keep up the tautness of mind, the high rage that fueled it, the extremity of emotion. Even back then I had to work hard to keep up that emotional tenor. I am frightened to even read from it out loud with this child in me. I do not want her to hear. I can scarcely believe I was once, and not so long ago, the person who wrote that book. When the (extensive) corrections to the galleys arrive for checking one final time I only glance at them with my side eyes.

I did my best. Especially considering part of me was never there for it. I knew even then that I was writing for the last time in a quaint and fast-waning tradition: the conventional novel. Well, conventional more or less.

Is it not the oddest combination of tenderness and resignation, the way I feel now?

I feel at last prepared, when the time comes, to die. I know it will be all right. God bathes us in hormones for death. Of this I am quite certain now. And protects us. As I am protected now. All worry has dissolved. I hover above the world without a care.

The quality of the fatigue, which is different than any other: the fatigue after hard work in the garden, or after swimming, or after writing, or the fatigue that comes with concern or worry. It is like none of those fatigues. And the quality of hunger—as if one is eating for one's very life. The urgency of the need for protein. These have both been revelations for me—but perhaps the most extraordinary of all is the quality of music. Listening today to *The Magic Flute.* Almost impossible. Unbearable in its beauty. Unable to contain my emotion I wept into my bathtub in Providence, where I sat trying to—what else—read student papers. I remember after Gary's death how it was nearly impossible to listen to music. Music too beautiful then, too, but in an entirely different way. That music should exist at all seemed an impossibility.

The swelling. The body begins to transform itself.

My life a transfigured rose.

You died at Saint Vincent's, and it is where I shall give birth. I have not walked into that hospital since the night I said goodbye before they took you away to be burned. I have been afraid many times in my life, but I have never been as afraid as that night. And how for a year afterwards I changed all walking routes so as not ever to have to pass that place. A little difficult with Angela there on Greenwich Avenue—still, I could not. Next week is the amnio and I will walk through those doors again. The same entry way—West Twelfth Street. How is it possible that so much sorrow and so much joy, and right up to the last moment, so much hope—can be held by that entryway? Eleven years separate the events. I still miss you. More than I can say.

I do feel a little better understanding that you were probably bathed in those death hormones. And that protection came. This has been a way back to you. We purposely chose Saint Vincent's. It is what I wanted.

Having conceived her, having kept her this long, I am home free, I tell myself. Foolish to think . . .

Here then my foolproof test for whether one is pregnant:

The inability to listen to Mozart.

The desire to wear nothing but cashmere.

Uncontrollable cravings for protein. Milk, cheese, beasts, egg-salad sandwiches. *Egg-salad sandwiches?*

I request that we not have lamb or veal for Christmas dinner. Just not in the mood to eat babies this year.

Emily, my niece, in fatigue moves toward the baby, flings herself on the belly—going back to the place of her making, toward the little one she was not so long ago. Her thumb in her mouth. Something I haven't seen her do in some time.

Although I love fish, not a morsel of fish since I have become pregnant has passed my lips. Christmas Eve and the traditional seven fish stare at me and I stare back. Is it the body rejecting the sea's impurities? Some sort of intelligence is at work, I guess. I do not question.

Never have I felt happier. Enjoying immensely my identification with the Virgin. Steve insists if anyone is capable of an Immaculate Conception . . . I quite like the idea.

Christmas Week.

A fluttering—without doubt. Small bird. A fluttering in the belly—strange motion. Late at night.

This life inside a life—now palpable in another way. Swim. Live.

A Dr. Seuss book to read to the child in utero—a gift. I think the only things I will be able to read to the baby are Gertrude Stein, Dr. Seuss, poetry, Beatrix Potter.

More green eggs and ham please! I request from the bed. Sam I am.

In the doctor's office today for a routine checkup. Fifth Avenue at Nineteenth Street. These precious days. Dr. Rehrer, very cool, low key, like a friend really. For Manhattan you are not even an old mother, she jokes. It will be fine. But she has been sick intermittently and hard to see. Now I see her partner, Dr. Dennis Matheson, most of the time. Everyone is relaxed over there. Happy to have babies around in every stage of becoming. The most natural thing in the world, he says.

I know that many women get a great dark stripe down their bellies when they are pregnant, and I request one please from Doctor M., but he just smiles. Not everyone, he informs me, gets one. Still, it is possible, of course, I tell him. I don't think so, he says, shaking his head.

Olivia, Helen's niece, on receipt of the news, joyously: "I know a beautiful name for a baby! *Kalina!*"

I think of the birth marked each year at this time. The amniocentesis next week. How can I summon the courage to know what to do if the results show a problem? The occurrence of Down's syndrome in women over thirty-five. I look at the graph. How it rises and rises every year after that. I must somehow prepare—even though I feel exempt, free from harm. Carrying this charm.

30 DECEMBER, TUESDAY

Quickly I walked through the entrance to Saint Vincent's. *Fear not,* he said. Fear not. Helen would be with me shortly—she had gone to park the car. Amnio today. It was snowing.

First we were ushered in to see the geneticist. I felt a little nervous, but not too nervous.

We were shown the chromosomes on film, which looked beautiful, translucent. We saw perfect ones, we saw defective ones—all beautiful I thought to myself. The counselor is as reassuring as possible. Sitting there I tried in different perfectly senseless ways to run the odds in my head. When I got home finally to my perfect sanctuary of worry I pored over the pregnancy books looking for hopeful things.

Dr. Mangano, who is, despite his name, Japanese, I think, performs a high-tech sonogram, and makes all kinds of measurements, takes all kinds of pictures. What a gorgeous sight. The spine like a fish bone. The great blossom, the bloom of the heart with its four chambers. Beating. It looks like a small bird in flight. Helen is holding my hand. First the baby is sucking its thumb. Then it seems to be waving. The doctor, as astounded as if this were the first time he was seeing a child in the womb. He stares, riveted. "What a beautiful—" he says, and then trails off, adjusting the focus.

"What a beautiful what?" we cry out.

"What a beautiful *brain!*"

Brain! We sigh.

"Look! Look!" he says, completely engrossed. "Would you like to know the sex?" Yes, we say, please, and it seems like forever before he says *he thinks* it's a girl. *He thinks it's a girl.* And at this news I begin to weep. Helen holds my hand. And such a pretty face. Look, he says, "she has a mouth like Brigitte Bardot." We stare incredulously into the shadows. *No!*

He takes an impossibly long needle that he will insert into my abdomen to get the amniotic fluid. I decide to look away. They will grow a few cells in a dish. Fingers, tiny hands, tiny feet, toes, lungs, bladder, a beautiful brain—we must wait six to ten days for the results. Just a few years ago it was more like a three-week wait. I imagine I'd be a basket case by then. I know in my heart of hearts that it will be fine—just as I knew all along that she was a girl. I buy a red rosary in the hospital gift shop.

We go to have Mexican food on Greenwich Avenue and begin to wait. I am supposed to remain fairly quiet. There is a slight risk of miscarriage as a result of the procedure. But I have seen her, and she has held on so fiercely, so tenaciously for so long. I visit Dixie in the afternoon—for luck.

Before the test there were papers to sign. As with everything there is a slight risk. Helen had been ready to march out of there. But I need to know. I have no idea what I would do. But I need to know.

Of course it is a girl—still, sometimes one's instincts let one down. Once I was immensely happy, it was a beautiful winter day in the city, I had just bought a new coat—when the phone rang. I could not have been more shocked. My sister Cathy in the hospital in Florida with a horrendously high fever. No one knows what it is. Toxic shock syndrome—before it had a name.

Maybe she will die. I sit in a stupor. She does not die, but I am never the same person after that.

Back to the country. I light church candles that say Santa Teresa.

I stare hour after hour into the Christmas tree. That piney, floating feeling. On the surface I am nervous, but at the center I am calm.

With that kind of fever the palms and the soles of the feet begin to peel. I remember this all of a sudden tonight.

One holds—one tries to hold the heart in abeyance until after the results of the amniocentesis.

Not possible.

I had read a book on how to conceive a girl. It had all made good sense. I believe in books. Once when I was dissatisfied with something about my swimming stroke, I got a book and read again and again the pertinent chapter, and *presto* it was fixed.

Most of my friends who have waited for children have boys. It comes from being overly attentive, overly conscientious, neurotic, over-anxious in the timing department. Too perfect, too desperate, too something. At any rate, it is possible a boy was never in the cards for me—I cannot conceive (pun intended) of having a boy. Still I am grateful for that book.

Though for a boy Beckett Kenneth was chosen as his name way in advance. Though I never said it out loud. Strange. For Samuel Beckett of course, and for my father.

I cannot lie down now without a cat draped over my belly. They must hear her or feel her heartbeat. They must smell the little varmint. This small beating sweet thing. Coco and then Fauve —they alternate, take turns. Purring and purring. And the baby moves.

I play her over and over in my mind. She is seven inches long. She has teeth. Her heart in flight. She is sucking her thumb. Then she is playing with her feet. Astounding does not begin to describe.

I call back those Italian charms—for what other word is there? Bagno Vignoli—those warm, fizzy, iridescent, luminous waters—a perfect blue-green. Those astounding mineral springs. And all the other charms of that most charmed trip.

The Poor Clares, scurrying through the dark streets.

The Piero de la Francescos.

Saint Francis.

A very quiet New Year's Eve. A glass of champagne. A tour of the night sky. A dark meditation on the baby's cells growing under glass. Tears.

The week I waited—from the last days of the dwindling year—waited in fog for the results of the amniocentesis. Descended into water. The mist I could not see my way through.

6 JANUARY, THE FEAST OF THE EPIPHANY

Still waiting for that last bit of news to be released from the amniotic fluid. Star, rose, snow. A private prayer. And then my litany of Hail Marys. I pray to the Virgin and keep wait as the Kings arrive.

8 P.M.

Helen, who has over so many years delivered so much news. Helen brightly calling out over the answering machine: *The baby is fine!*

Never known such happiness.

I call my parents: *She is perfect.*

I close my eyes now and see the ferocity of the image on the screen. The will at all costs to live. Without knowledge of what that is. I feel the pure life force, pounding in me.

15 JANUARY

Having decided to wait until after the amnio to tell most people, more and more now know. How I long already for those days when it was mine—my secret, and the two of us would walk—to class, to readings, in silence, in innocence. Or go for a swim.

I am really beginning to swell now. There really wouldn't have been much more time for the two of us alone in this, after all—without anyone knowing. Still wanting to preserve what we had together just a moment longer—isn't that always what I wanted, longed for—*one more minute.*

The joy now unalloyed. The days pass blissfully. I work on *The Bay of Angels* a little and dream.

Still on Christmas break. Louis and Louise come for a visit. We go back to their house. I am up here alone. Helen at work in the city. They pamper me. Cook me comforting dinners. We chat by candlelight—these precious nights—until I begin to shut my eyes. Louis walks me to my door. We have started calling each other Hansel and Gretel. We are dwarfed by the forest, a little lost. He takes my arm. He assures me it will be OK. Throws breadcrumbs.

I go back to Saint Vincent's for a follow-up sonogram. Again measurements of all sorts are made. The length of the arm from the elbow to the wrist—that sort of thing. The heart beating on the screen. It looks like a bird in flight, they say, and it is true. The heart spreading its wings.

The heart like a cat's paw or a rose opening.

Very happy to imagine having this baby in my neighborhood. After twenty years here—this is the last thing I might have expected . . . Always believed deep down that I would never have a child.

Once I had planned to marry, believing that it was the only way. The conventions of my mother. Hearing them all too loudly in my head. *Get married.* Why does everyone always assume that what was right for them would be right for anyone else? No matter how happy they are? I was far too young at any rate. Had not even written *Ghost Dance* yet. He was the most lovely of men. Helen and I heartbroken, resigned. The life we had. *Maybe it is best—if you really want a child . . .* But mine is an intelligence so impossibly oriented toward self-preservation that I cannot go through with it. I did not know this before I took it that far. I did not know. I did not mean to hurt him—or anyone. I wonder where he is today. I know he's published a few books. I know his father died.

I have not thought of this in twenty years, and yet here it is back tonight. A scene for a film I wrote when I first moved to the city. A woman who is going increasingly mad (but no one can be sure of it until this scene) believes she is nine months pregnant and about to have a baby, but she has no swollen belly whatsoever, no physical manifestation of her pregnancy. It was how I mourned the idea of never having children, I think. I knew I was not going to ever become a writer if I had them then, and I assumed, in those days, that if I waited until after, should I ever actually become a writer, it would be far, far too late. Written in 1978.

On the other hand I wrote a little screenplay—a relief from the sorrow of the novels—in 1993 about a universe of women, and of one woman in particular who is pregnant. The last line: *It's a girl!*

I send supplies to her through the placenta. The placenta, as it turns out, performs the functions of the adult lungs, kidneys, intestines, liver, and some of the hormone glands. It combats infections. Within it CO_2 leaves the baby's bloodstream and is exchanged for oxygen brought by the mother's bloodstream through her lungs across the porous walls of the closed blood vessels. No wonder I can't breathe. No wonder I am so tired.

It is nice at least to have a reason for this fatigue—which Dr. R. promised would go away but has not yet.

I dream of the cord filled with blood like a garden hose. The light bluish green gel that shines through the pale sheath. Glistening. Its swimming-pool light. In my mind it is remarkably beautiful. In fact I cannot imagine a more beautiful thing.

This pregnancy calling up all the other moments of bliss. Swimming at the health club in Cape Cod every day. Almost no one else in the pool. That feeling. The light streaming through the glass roof in winter. Each time I turn my head for a breath and lift my arm I see a piece of the sky. Blue with clouds. A little bit of paradise. I am writing *AVA* with every stroke. I remember thinking then I am living my life exactly, exactly as I have always wanted to.

Blood travels at four miles an hour and completes the round trip through the cord in only thirty seconds. All that moves in me. No wonder I am light-headed.

I worry about telling my sister Christine about the baby—as I do not want to hurt her any more than she has already been hurt. I consider getting her a new kitten in preparation for the news. She probably will not have children. She feels as if she has missed out on everything on account of her illness. I have had bouts of the same thing—but without the intensity, or relentlessness—without the degree. I love her. More than she can know.

All that has always moved in me.

No American breasts are allowed out under any circumstances in the 1950s—that would have given women too much power and disrupted the societal order too extremely—breasts are just too sexual, too threatening, just too too—the entire society geared toward the feelings of men. So I am formula-fed, "better than breast milk" the doctors bragged back then. The fools. Arrogance of the 1950s. And as a result I am colicky and miserable for a whole year.

Most men have found me a little intimidating for a variety of reasons, but now it is exaggerated. *Exactly where did you get that baby?* they ask nervously.

Brown quibbles with me about pay for my sabbatical and has no official policy on maternity leave. All a little outrageous for such a self-proclaimed bastion of liberal thinking. In my exhaustion they attempt to bargain with me. *Very tricky.* I have to begin imagining a plan of escape. They might have been more grateful for these three years of servitude—directing a whole creative writing program for God's sake—a preposterous notion. I wore the hostess crown most reluctantly. On occasion even displayed bad manners. Handled the administration without grace or flare. Not made for it. It was only the students I ever felt comfortable championing and protecting.

20 JANUARY

Talked to Judith. She is decidedly sadder, more vulnerable, since Zenka's death. I hear the solitude in her voice. She is in London now. I speak back double-voiced, the child's voice speaking with mine, and I wonder if this is somehow painful for her to hear. She has always been a great advocate for children. Zenka, on the other hand, I can still hear her: *never, never, never!* But Judith is pleased. I had told her first, before just about anyone, when the news was only a few days old and all we could do was hope. She was making her first trip to New York City. We sat next to one another at the White Horse Tavern—a place she insisted on going. "Dylan's pub." *I am having a baby.* And she in response: *You will teach the rest of the world how to live.*

And on another occasion: *You always know in the end what to do. If you are doing it it must be exactly the right thing. And others will flock to copy you.* I miss them both every day. *Come stay in Tourettes,* she says. *The babies drink wine with their water and they stay up all night!*

Semitic blood intermingling with my own now to create this little being. Two great religions meeting in my body. On both sides there are survivors. From both World Wars. Armenian, Jewish. She shall be some child.

The tenacity of the born.
The tenacity of the unborn.

The impossibility of having a child—I began believing it was not to occur—I had done nothing toward making it occur, and I found that to be significant.

Take loving note—for you have never seen this curve, this swell before in your body—and you shall never see it again.

The most alarming failure of imagination—that I never dreamt I could ever feel this way.

Embryo from the Greek, to swell.

The embryo floats in its amniotic envelope.

A gift unanticipated—this ability to simply shed all that once disturbed so. My war with the literary mainstream ended. I have no desire to press against them. It is part of this great letting go now. It clears the path for me at forty-two to begin my real work, my real writing. I needed it once, I suppose, in order to grow, to keep my edge, to push myself, to write up against. A way of clarifying, even defining my intentions. But no longer. It was part of my apprenticeship. Useful. It served its purpose well. It is, I must say, a strange feeling to be at last ready to write something finally of my own. After all this time.

It's lovely to be in this gorgeous fog carrying all this miraculousness inside.

Provincetown in winter. I was writing *AVA*, surrounded by ocean. And another winter there grieving—as alive as I would ever be—and trying to write *The Art Lover.* Failing at everything, it seemed. Still I felt the hard work of living, the cost of loving too much. This flood of hormones. I'm waking up at odd hours now—wide awake, sitting straight up in bed and worrying about the strangest things. Dreamt I drowned in the bay at night. A small circle of friends trying to resuscitate. I could see them from on high. Don't even bother trying, I instruct them serenely.

There were in fact papers to sign on that amniocentesis table before the procedure. Some risk of miscarriage. Are you sure you want to do this? Helen asks. She is ready to pack us up and get out of there. Yes, I am sure, I say, though I don't on reflection have any real idea why I am sure. Something is protecting me. I am as calm as I have ever been, will ever be. It will be OK, I said that day, and squeezed her hand.

The hospital after the months and months of Gary's dying a familiar place. Strangely I am glad to be back in the intensity of the emotion, the pain I felt back then. If I could live through that . . . It has given me a crazy courage. A weird fearlessness. Since that day, 1 October 1986, I have lived a free person.

The worst possible thing had already happened, so what else was there to fear?

That was twelve, thirteen years ago now. Afterwards I left for the Fine Arts Work Center in Provincetown. Never had the desire been so great as then to have a baby. Replace, replace, as if one could. That year for my birthday Helen got me a blue Maine coon cat. I was working on *The Art Lover*; I named him Fauve.

Most lovely of purring consolations. How I wept and held him tightly to me and kissed him around the collar.

Wanting a baby so much. Of course it would have been the wrong time. It did not happen then. Though it seemed the only thing that might mend me.

Someone to be there once the absences began to accumulate.

How to redeem the saddest of childhoods? How to become a mother when she had none?

She became a super mom. She gave us everything. Smothered with attention and love. Too much? Who can say? As a result of being over-loved I have become the person I am today. With little concern for other's approval or acceptance. Little desire to fit in—an extraordinary gift, that freedom.

My father once said that my mother was never more happy than when she was pregnant—or more beautiful.

I feel claustrophobic. That the two of us can't do this together anymore. Share the same body. I want to throw myself from my tiny attic garret onto Waterman Street and have it be over. I can't breathe.

We are two hearts, four arms, four legs, two brains, four eyes, in one body. It's the oddest thing. I don't know how I'm supposed to walk around and go to school and act like an ordinary person.

As if I were not strange enough already—now, this eight-chambered heart.

The abundance of love I have always felt. Surfeit of emotion—now focused. An unborn music.

Such expectation.

The demands of love. Having poured it into my books without hesitation, only to find on completion that I had been refilled again.

Duras, *Le Camion*: "She might have said straight off there is no story outside love."

Pregnancy. The attempt in part to keep the deaths of those one loves at bay. And in the case of the dead, to bring back—somehow.

Sat on a panel in Boston about the usual thing—writing on the fringe, breaking the rules. A little tedious in the end . . . My mind's a blur these days. Increasingly I can't remember things. A strange sensation—as if I were sloughing off all but the essential. And yet would I retain even the essential, I wonder? When members of the audience asked questions of us, their panel, I found it necessary to write the question down, because if another panelist answered first, I didn't have a clue what it was I was supposed to talk about. *Shouldn't one learn to write traditionally first?*—that sort of thing. I dislike making public pronouncements (though I've made plenty), but with my weird amnesia and laissez-faire attitude I felt little pain—well, less pain than usual. I am feeling increasingly free of everything that has constricted. That has conspired to keep me caged. Including myself. Amazing.

Dixie was there taking photos of my ever-evolving shape. Dixie, that sweet documenter. We drove back to Providence afterwards. I stretched out in the back seat happy as a cat.

I am at that stage where people politely notice that I have gained a lot of weight, but they are not quite sure I am pregnant. I blurt it out now at every turn: *I am having a baby in June!*

A panel at Columbia a few weeks earlier after which I swore I would never do one of these things again. So why do I? I imagine with a child all that is extraneous or false or simply silly will fall away. One can only hope.

I am struck at how engrossed I am in every detail of the pregnancy itself and yet have thought very little about the end result. Sometimes I think that after the nine months I will be finished, I will have accomplished a very great thing—and then it will be done. But of course, as everyone is all too happy to remind me, it will only be the beginning. The child at this point is still very, very abstract. I don't know a thing about having a baby around. Not really. Not where I am the one *in charge.* But the pregnancy is so mesmerizing and I fall into simply taking it day by day. I will deal with the child once there *is* one. For now though I find that it is passing suddenly all too quickly and I want to slow it down, to stay in this, to prolong these feelings. Harbor, vessel, rose.

2 FEBRUARY—FIVE MONTHS

What moves inside my motion?

What beats so fiercely, insistently, saying *here, here, I am here.*
Love does, love does, love does.

Thinking of Judith and Zenka again. All our feelings so much on the surface—we cannot help it. Flirting together. They seventy and seventy-five at the time. How they protected me when they could—that terrible and wonderful summer. Rolling in sweet herbs with the next beautiful boy—feeling the end of all things. Waiting to get well. Having ended our life together, this time for good. Oh, Helen. Or so I thought. That autumn of the pot-au-feu. They held my hands. We gossiped about everyone and everything. We dreamt each day of how I might stay forever. I could take care of their dog, Rimbaud, while they were away. Swerving through the streets protected by that soulful golden retriever. Always another tearful good-bye at the airport in Nice. Always another joyful reunion at that same airport. Later the sadnesses would be in London—one of those British taxis—a cab ride in the rain. I remember thinking I had never seen such roses. This through terrible sorrow. Somehow London seemed an apt place to be sad.

The last time I had been there. Walking into that flat in Roehampton. We brought Zenka a birthday present from Paris. Two French engravings: Spring, Winter. Helen and I had come for the day, taking the Chunnel. We ate Indian food. At every table talk of the mad cow.

I direct the creative writing program as if I were Francis Coppola directing a film from his isolation chamber. It's kind of wonderful to be so strangely free of the politics, the thousand discontents, the problems at every turn. This will be my last year as director. I must say I have not been exactly suited for the task—and now—I move through the days as if in a dream. Turning inward, sending forth instructions through a tiny microphone in my throat. Even a weirder director than before. If that's possible.

Harboring a miracle, who can speak of mundane things? Though I know this is the most everyday and ordinary of miracles—or so they say. I can't believe so many women have had children and so many seem rather blasé about the whole thing. Most people's only contact with the sublime. Or perhaps they simply do not speak of such things in their conscious waking life, in which a hundred other obligations obscure the fact. Or they have put it aside. Or, as so many have put it: childbirth—a misery to be endured.

Someone tells me an outlandish story about a friend who schedules C-sections for herself in order to be spared the whole ordeal of birth. What is the word for the deliberate cutting off in oneself of those experiences that are potentially most profound in order to be spared pain? There must be a word in English, as it seems a particularly American trait.

And while we're at it, what is the word in American for the similar phenomenon of deliberately cutting off a dream or potential for the simple reason that it is not profitable?

I am astounded to imagine what magic a woman's body is capable of. Though I always suspected . . . Of course somewhere I always knew.

Always in the back of my mind the notion that I could still miscarry even if a charmed star hung over me on the night of her conception. Most unlikely and precious night.

A flood of blood—the only way to prepare—as I do in dreams —should something go wrong.

Always knew I wanted to have the experience of pregnancy. I am too much body to have missed out on such an event. *Maso* is flesh in Slovak, a lover once told me.

That extreme winter of vodka and snow and oblivion. His cigarettes and cynicism. He was a kind man. And I was wild back then.

He hurt me terribly and possibly inadvertently a few years back and we parted ways. I miss him.

When I write every day I never remember my dreams. But now that the writing has become sporadic, my dreams come streaming back. They are not altogether welcome, I might add.

She turns from amphibian to fish to bird to person.

I grow happily, happily rotund. I negotiate the curves gracefully.

This for me feels like a natural state. The easy happiness that has always, always eluded me. My intensities smoothed over a little. The sorrow modulated.

This peace. My friends, who have watched me struggle for years trying to think of ways to make money while I wrote, say, had you known, you could have been a surrogate mother every year, and written to your heart's content. And have been well.

In another life I might have had five children, like my mother. But I do not have another life. And I miss writing. Nothing, not even this, can take its place. That dark radiance. It is as beautiful as anything I have ever known. It brings me to a place of unearthly happiness. I have not forgotten . . .

Who could she have spoken to about that flood of feelings? Or about her growing body? Or her fears? Having already had two miscarriages. How could she not have believed it was just a part of the sorrow that seemed to follow her. *The saddest of all childhoods.* Mother. She rarely spoke of it. But the illness and death of one's mother at a young and crucial age must mark forever the way the world is experienced. A sorrowful place. Where was the solace? My father—yes, in part. Her religion. But who could she really speak to about these matters? Her sister? We were company, she said that more than once. Her brood of children. But how were we company? I think of her otherworldly isolation. And yet it is true she was always utterly present with us. So much so that each of us felt like an only child. How is it possible?

To write without embellishment. Without concern for the larger shapes. To simply record. And to have that be enough. That I was here. And that this, this most extraordinary and ordinary thing, happened to me once. It seems in this state more possible to do this than ever before. To just be. And write from there. Without grander schemes or plans for the text. Another freedom. To enjoy it as long as it lasts. It won't last forever of course. Relish it.

Meanwhile Frida languorously waits. So unlike me to have lost the compulsion to compose at that level. It's part of the letting go. Even the things that are most pressing or most dear become a little lost—not in a bad way.

This is the story of two souls in transit: the music of the spheres—

Provincetown, the dunes: I am walking through drifts and drifts of sand toward the ocean, aware of its presence, surrounded by it, caressed by it, the feel of it, the smell—and yet it is some distance away, still out of reach.

I offend some of those friends who have neglected to have children, in ways I naively could not have predicted. *Who do you think you are?* I serve as a painful reminder. Time passes. And all opportunity. Everything is ephemeral, fleeting—over before we know it.

The ocean in winter. How Ilene and I let it ravage us. Years ago already. Will we have children? we wondered over the riot of surf. Yes. Maybe. We were like schoolgirls together. A little shy. Whispering in the dark, every hope, every fear. Almost every fear.

I tell her about the baby. She is more thrilled than anyone, it seems. She has a five-year-old son and is somewhat lonely in it. I will be company—and she for me. It's possible this child will bring us back together—as was always meant to be.

8 FEBRUARY, VERMONT STUDIO CENTER

Wishing in summer for the negative numbers, attracted to the below zero, I agreed to come up here near the Canadian border for a week of teaching. Careful of the ice. I work hard and try to stay focused on the student papers. Also need to complete an essay for Jason. I must say I'm not sure I have the powers of concentration. I'll just have to let that dictate the way the piece goes. What are my choices? I don't know why I agree ever to write an essay. I always suffer them—though I'm happy after they are done to have a record of sorts of the person I once was. I've gotten a second wind this trimester, which is a lucky thing since there is a lot of work to do up here.

I resist reading *Defiance* out loud. Not in front of the one who is still forming. The book feels that visceral, that poisonous to me. The pages burn in my hands. It broke my heart to write. Unlike any of the other books. A harrowing process. I don't want her to hear my voice spitting out those grim syllables.

Usually I get a little crazy around the time a book is coming out—but it's different this time. I am not really so invested in it. It will be out in May and I will be eight months pregnant. This will preclude my traveling to "promote" it and nothing could make me happier. It is an undue burden I usually feel compelled to take on. Sorry, not this time. A great excuse—no airplane will carry me in the eighth month of pregnancy. *Quelle dommage!* I must say it does now feel like the pregnancy has taken—and that there will actually be a baby. I know there are premature births and every other kind of mishap still to move through—but I'm not worried anymore. And *Defiance?* It is a tough book. It can take care of itself.

At what week is the baby viable?

It presents itself as an angular shape in my mind—the next

corner to turn. I try to prepare myself for the next possible thing and then the next, every step of the way. Premature birth.

Late in the seventh month you are viable, I have found out.

Steve Moore, my former editor at Dalkey Archive, calls her Baby Defiance.

Those my age, in serious mid-life crisis mode, their children grown, look at me a bit bewildered. To have gone about this in such a strange fashion. But to have had children young—for me it seemed not unimaginable, but simply not possible. The kind of mother I would have been back then: resentful, depressed, detached, enraged, indifferent.

"What *is* known is that she liked and was good at talking to children (there are many witnesses to this), that she often bitterly regretted not having them, and that she never consoled herself with the belief that her books were a substitute or an equivalent. These feelings would surface whenever she was depressed. In her deepest plunges into 'melancholy' or a sense of failure, she always uttered the words 'children': 'It's having no children,' it's 'a desire for children.'"

—from the Hermione Lee biography of Virginia Woolf

"I put my life blood into writing, she (Vanessa) had children."

To wait—it was not such a calculated risk, considering the options. All along I was willing to forgo it all entirely. It is why I am so good at getting jobs, I think: I am perfectly content not to have the job at all.

Once, when I was sure I was pregnant and far too young to consider such a thing but dreaded the options, Helen said, We do not have to decide right away, and she took me to a Yankees game—an oddly consoling thing—and held my hand. The father a good friend of ours. She had known about the affair.

How have we made it through all these years? Mutual respect comes to mind. Flexibility. Devotion.

Two souls in transit.

The ability to change everything and at the last minute if necessary. Autumn. A walk on the Poet's Walk. We are going to have a baby!

All those years of my youth working those terrible temporary jobs in all those law firms for all those idiotic lawyers and slowly, slowly dying. Those years when all I could do it seemed was weep.

In the eighth inning, she says, maybe we could have the child.

Are people from unhappy or broken families constantly trying to remake, retrieve, make whole, complete? Maybe we could have the child, once, she said.

I felt my early life to be completely smothered by my mother's children. Though I was never asked to take care of them. Still, there was always so much commotion. I had to go far and live long to want to have a child of my own.

At the top of the ninth—Helen, I don't think so.

My mother—*the saddest of childhoods*—and her five little ones.

Virginia Woolf: "I shall make myself face the fact that there is nothing—nothing for any of us. Work, reading, writing, all are disguises; and relationships with people. Yes, even having children would be useless." —*A Writer's Diary*

A while back when we were in one of our efficient phases, we made an appointment with a fancy lawyer to handle the legal aspects of having a child. She was big deal—had represented Hedda Nussbaum, all kinds of characters. She decided to read *The American Woman in the Chinese Hat* and told Helen that even though she knew it was fiction she felt concerned about *my ability to be a mother*. Perhaps, when the time came, the baby *might need some representing. Protection.* That I already had a very, very dim view of lawyers could not prepare me for her stupidity, or her arrogance.

Intrigued by every single moment of this—even the frightening parts as they come. There is always some terror. Of course. Loving every aspect of being pregnant is an odd thing. Not used to such simple happiness—not since childhood at any rate. It all comes back. The dark afternoons of music. Ballet lessons three times a week with that marvelous diva Irene Fokine. In the summer I took painting lessons. My brother and I played Scrabble for hours and hours on the dock of my grandparents' lake house.

I really do glow. Happily, happily sitting on my nest.

The baby moving inside. A foot. A fist. An elbow perhaps. A fin.

Accretion of the days. To attend to every trembling, every motion.

I am a novelist in part because I love the long haul, my stamina is of the long-distance sort. In the pool I am best after the first fifteen laps. I believe in relationships for life. Things cut off abruptly shock my system badly. Only once did I have to end something in that way. The obsession on both sides over time had grown monstrous. Finally there was no other option. It took years to recover.

It is a little disconcerting to have those friends who did not have children—those who made that decision, those who had counted me among them, one of the childless—to turn away now, if only slightly.

Disregarding what one gives up for this. Seeing it as only rosy, and resenting it.

On the street some women avert their eyes when they see me. I am a reminder of what they have failed to do. I sympathize,

I really do. But I, for better and worse, have always been a person who acts on my impulses. Because, for the most part, I am someone incapable of living with regret.

Action, driven as much by intuition as by reason. I have always been amused by the yuppies, who think they might open some sort of ledger and see if there was enough money yet, enough "quality time." And a nursery school and college lined up. We'd better get on a waiting list!

Children cannot be thought through—could not for me at any rate. The logical conclusion would have been no.

Dear Douglas Culhane. His role in all of this never to be forgotten or underestimated. How he made the desire for the child precise. Brought it to full cognizance. The strange workings of this world. Douglas was wonderful in all ways.

I might say more but am reluctant to invade his privacy. The particular dangers of keeping a journal that others might see. A suspect project in many ways.

Also not to forget the Quiet Monsieur, as we called him, standing discreetly in the corner. His favorite color is red. His favorite animal, a dog. He admires most, fidelity. I am speaking in code a little, because I feel I must. He was all in all a perfect little gentleman.

Drunk at a dinner party, our eyes mistakenly meet and we forget for a moment that we do not love each other anymore.

Granted, it has not always been easy.

Not always such smooth sailing.

This struggle against ruin. This vote, as Louis says, for the future—this infinitesimal gesture—against the vanishing.

Once a crimson wreath . . . I shall carry it the rest of my life.

Language is a rose and the future is still a rose, opening.

Unable to hold on to them I watch them age. All acts of retrieval doomed. I remember that late fall afternoon in the woods near the MacDowell Colony where my parents and I walked and walked and grew increasingly lost—those mortal woods.

14 FEBRUARY

Last night my back to the utterly black living room and the feeling is—what? That everything is about to be taken away. One of us, or both. Helen making a Valentine's Day dinner. I sitting by the fire.

Ah, the old terror returns.

My idols, my models, the ones I respect most: Woolf, Beckett, Stein—all childless.

"From that day forth things went from bad to worse, to worse and worse. Not that she neglected me enough, but the way she kept plaguing me with *our* child, exhibiting her belly and breasts and saying it was due any moment, she could feel it lepping already. If it's lepping, I said, it's not mine."

—*Samuel Beckett,* FIRST LOVE

17 FEBRUARY

Emily, six years old today, wanted to replay the details of her birth. I was not there. I was teaching in Illinois that year. The most awful of winters and how I kept having to fly home. The worst of all times for our family. My sister in labor for days it seemed. Emily followed me around the birthday party feeding me sweet things because she'd heard that might make the baby move. Her little hand on my belly. She says Sally and Julianna are her favorite names.

From the March *Vanity Fair*: "Michael L. tells Pisces to expect at least one more miracle . . . With Jupiter in your sign all this year, such a miracle is destined to happen at least once more."

I feel like a planet these days. Some heavenly body. Hauling the universe and stars. Floating into every room.

Making a mysterious music.

My students say that when I speak it is as if I am lit from within.

The eight chambers of these two hearts pumping blood.

The gush. I have never felt so flush with blood. I hear it in my ears.

It makes a clanging sound.

One does glow as a result. Luminous in the dark. Like those paper planets at that store on Broadway, Star Magic.

Not without its wonder and terror.

Language is a rose and the future is still a rose opening.

Jason leaves a message. "I hope you are well and the one traveling with you."

25 FEBRUARY

Remember man that you are dust and unto dust you shall return.

Ash placed on my high forehead. I remember her perfect forehead from the sonogram. Next year the child's forehead will have emerged, that extraordinary curve—*we are ash*—lest we forget.

It is when the church is refreshingly direct that I find it most convincing. My sister informs me that they are even waffling on Hell now.

Great solitude now. Largely of the thrilling kind. It's as if I were sitting in a dark theater alone right before the film starts. The second row. Waiting. One of the headiest pleasures in this world.

I turn inward now.

The room lit by roses.

Concentrate on the baby. Feel the ferocity of the life force, the tenacity, the insistence to live. One feels the child's single goal now—to be born.

A great throbbing inside.

In a daydream I will the car to swerve—to go up in a blaze—before it all begins.

But immediately after I think—one day we will have to get her a Volvo—something in which to survive the crashes when they come. I have always imagined myself in a black Saab. Yes, perhaps we will have a black Saab.

The double life pounding in me. The two life intensities. It's almost unbearable at times. All this life. All this living.

Helen, as always, amazing in her flexibility, generosity, open-mindedness, devotion. Ready to change course, think again, re-imagine. A capacity almost no one else I know has. Not to that degree. It makes what is to come all the more exhilarating, exciting, new.

9 MARCH

Never shall there be another day like this, not ever again in my life. My birthday.

Two lives. One birth celebrated, memorialized. One anticipated, about to be.

To finally understand "tears of joy."

I am told I look ten years younger since I have become pregnant. A lucky thing given my age. I have friends, I have a younger brother with children in college.

Fertility, ripeness, how to describe the readiness that took over me? I cannot in any way account for it.

Mainstream heterosexual breeding sorts try to invite me into their club now. *I don't think so.*

So much freedom and bliss. I feel completely liberated—that I have done this thing, and on my own terms.

My mother's one request: that one day before she dies I write a happy book. This must be that book. Maybe I will publish it after all.

I am home sick from school. Not really too sick, just a little sick. Juices and sodas—plenty of fluids. Pastina and broth, my mother brings. I am thrilled to have her so nearby all day long.

And to myself, more or less. The baby is taking a nap. School is such a bore. I hate having to go. I've got my little sick station set up on the couch. My private universe of crayons and paper and music and TV and books. Nothing makes me happier.

The failure of public education to work. In my case, certainly in my case. A sorrow to this day. The waste of so much potential for good.

Xui-Di says in China eggs are hoarded for the pregnant women.

This must explain my overwhelming desire for egg-salad sandwiches, something I have not eaten in thirty years probably.

14 MARCH

The nest outside the bathroom window fills with snow.

As always I play music day and night and wonder if this in any way shall effect the course of this baby's life.

There is no money, only temp jobs, no health insurance, only a tiny rented apartment. No possibility of a child here—I cannot even keep myself together—for many, many years. When I take my first real job I am already thirty-five. At my wit's end by then. There is no money, not for a long time, only, after a while, these books. So much hard-earned joy. To live without regret—regardless of the other consequences. Without my writing there would have been no life for me. It's all too clear.

16 MARCH

Trimester three! Twenty-seven weeks! Yipee!

Leslie Hill, on naming, from *Beckett's Fiction* : "Foisted on me by others, the name is an imposition and a falsehood, spelt or written by myself alone, it names me with radical singularity."

Yes, the predicament of the name. I have never once felt that Carole Maso is my real name. I wonder if anyone else feels this way.

From another notebook altogether. From another zone of the brain. From *The Bay of Angels:*

I named my child Mercy, Lamb.

Seraphina, the burning one.

I named my child The One Who Predicts the Future, though I never wanted that.

I named my child Pillar, Staff.

Henry, from the Old High German *Haganrih*, which means ruler of the enclosure, how awful.

I named my baby Plum, Pear Blossom, Shining Path.

I named my child Rose Chloe—that's blooming horse. I almost named her Rose Seraphina, and that would have been a horse that burns.

I named her Kami, which is tortoise, the name denotes long life.

Kameko—tortoise child.

Kameyo—tortoise generation.

So she might have a long life.

And Tori—turtle dove.

I named my child Sorrow, inadvertently, I did not mean to. In the darkness, Rebecca—that is noose, to tie or bind. In the gloom I named my baby Mary—which means bitter, but now I name my child Day and Star and Elm Limb. I named my child Fearlessness so that she might never be frightened. An Offering of Songs.

Vigilant was the name of my child.

I named my baby Many Achievements, Five Ravens, Red Bird. I named her Goes Forth Bravely. Beautiful Lake. Shaking Snow, Red Echo, Walking by the River.

I named my child War, by mistake. That would be Marcella or Martine. I named my child Ulric—Wolf Power. Oh my son! After awhile though I wised up and passed on Brunhilde, Helmut, Hermann, Walter. And Egon—the point of the sword. I do not value power in battle and so skipped over Maude.

Instead I named my child Sibeta—the one who finds a fish under a rock. I named my child Miraculous. Sacred Bells and Ray of Light. And Durga—Unattainable. Olwynn—White Footprint. And Monica—solitary one. I named my child Babette, that is stranger. I named her Claudia—lame—without realizing it.

How are you feeling, Ava Klein?

I named my child Perdita, does that answer your question?

I named my child Thirst. And Miriam—Sea of Sorrow, Bitterness. And Cendrine—that's Ashes. I named my child Bitterness, but I am feeling better now, thank you. I named my child God Is With Thee, though I do not feel Him.

I named her Isolde—Ruler of Ice. Giselle, which is pledge and hostage.

Harita, a lovely name, derived from the Sanskrit, denotes a color of yellow, green, or brown, a monkey, the sun, the wind, and several other things.

I named her Sylvie so that she would feel at home in the sunless forest and then handed her over to the Madame so she might live. Placed in the basket or pea pod or a hat box for now. Hidden in the goose egg, the walnut shell, the plum for now. I named her Bethany—House of Figs. I named her Lucia to protect her from the dark. Dolpin, Lion. Phillipa—lover of horses. I named her Daughter of the Oath. I gave her away. So she might live.

I named her Clothed in Red, because for nine months I never stopped bleeding. Xing, which is star. I named her Good-bye for Now. I named my son Yitzchak—that's He Will Laugh. And Isiah, Salvation.

How are you feeling, Ava Klein?

I named him Salvation. And Rescue

And Bela derived from a word that means wave, or a word that means time, or a word that means limit. It is also indicative of a type of flower, or a violin.

As for me? I might have been named Song of Joy. I might have been named The Lover of Flowers. As it is, I was named Bird. And what could be lovelier than that?

I named my daughter Arabella—Beautiful Altar, and Andromeda—The Rescued One.

I named my daughter Esme, the past participle of the verb to love. I named her She Has Peace, and Shining Beautiful Valley, and Farewell to Spring . . .

The ticket man at the train station in Providence asks where I am going—a perfectly reasonable question, in fact his job, but I could not for the life of me remember. I forget my purse. I lose my bank card, my keys. Maybe it's time to start working from home now. The absent-minded professor indeed.

It was Stamford, Connecticut, I was going to. After a few moments it came back. To meet Helen and then go up to the house. One time in fall Laura too was at that station to greet me. How much I miss her. Sequestered out there in Colorado, the Hate State. I am hoping Laura will come here before too long. I want her to be with me pregnant. I'm not sure though. I sense her ambivalence. I pray she does not defect—she is one of the people I can least afford to lose.

A few nights of the same nightmare: I go to sleep seven months pregnant, I wake up and my stomach is flat, the baby gone. No explanation. As if it is completely normal. As if I had only imagined it, as if I was crazy all along.

A weird delirium. Ghost images from my past. As if my life were over. A man who came one night up the rickety sea-soaked steps. The foghorns, the fog, this rolling, oceanic body. A most memorable time . . . He left his footprints in ice the next morning. By noon they were gone. I never saw him again.

I am filled with presence and spirit. It is impossible to ignore now. This boisterous other soul, making herself known. Taking my thoughts, my thinking away.

This motion within my motion. This pulsing within my pulse.

In the train station in Hudson on my way to the city. Just called Louis and Louise to go check on the house because I am quite certain I have left the candles on. Visions of the whole beloved house in ashes. Oh, the intensity and blur of these days. So much hope and desire it frightens me.

In pregnancy it seems the candles are always burning.

Turning forty, two years ago. Assessing my life. My only regret —that I had not had a child.

In me, the refusal to refuse joy. To refuse one single thing. Tempered a little since I have gotten older. Not to cause others undue sorrow, pain anymore. Still, it is how I choose to live.

Not sure I would advise anyone to wait until after forty if there was a choice. The statistics daunting. The quality of the worry. The personal implications—*what kind of mother are you anyway?*

High risk.

18 MARCH

The first glucose test is a little off and so I must go for the three-hour glucose tolerance test, a more refined picture of what's up. I've always had small problems with sugar and so assume this test will show the need to change my diet or something. Also my sister, pregnant with Emily, failed this one. Off then to the lab.

East Village, 10 A.M.

I down the awful ten-ounce sweet drink and feel the little one doing somersaults, cartwheels—incredible dizziness, headache.

The baby going wild. I can hardly write this sentence. Sickness.

At half-hour intervals the technician comes for blood . . .

I'm feeling better the further I get away from the sweet now and can better watch the comings and goings in the lounge.

I walk a blind man to the blood lab. There's a young Latino man here to get a drug test. He comes once a month with his drug counselor. He is an assistant teacher now and the kids like him. He has fed the children and they are now having their naps. He likes to take them to Central Park. To the Bronx Zoo. To New Jersey, where they have ants and termites. That's what he says to his counselor, who just sits there exhausted-looking.

A father and little boy walk in. Blood is taken from the father's arm. When he returns the son asks him, "Are you still strong?"

Parole officers fight with their parolees. "I'm just doing my job, man."

"You're trying to take my children away."

"I'm just doing my job."

The distance from the sweet.

People who need blood levels taken coming in and out all day—bipolars and so forth.

I'm feeling a little disoriented from all the stimulus. Every one of these people was born. Was someone's baby. I could weep at the thought of it.

My mother entering the room with a bowl of pastina. Home from school. The tyrants silenced.

Say you are still strong.

Before I even have a sufficient chance to worry about anything Helen calls, once more with her good news: "Your blood sugar is normal."

21 MARCH

The sound of my heart and my blood, and all day nothing but Bach. His birthday (313 years).

It's the claustrophobia that's a little difficult. The pancakes on the plate are too crowded. The books on the bookshelves make me crazy. There's no bed big enough.

When I think of how trouble-free this pregnancy has been. Especially remembering everyone else's stories. No nausea, no bleeding, no backaches, no headaches, no swollen legs—in fact my back has never felt better—it must be the new distribution of weight.

Also I am not in the least squeamish or hypochondriacal or neurotic about the workings of my body, and this goes a long way when pregnant.

Fear that the good feeling cannot last, will not.

And it has been a bliss, intellectually as well—loving as I do the place of all potential. Before anything that is going to happen has happened yet.

I put the little tape player next to my belly and play the *Clarinet Quintet in A Major* for her. I can listen to Mozart again. The gift that is Mozart.

I'm more and more tired now again.

I see myself from far off. I see myself from the future. My life over. "During that time she traveled by train often . . . "

From *The Bay of Angels:*
Sophie sees a stork go by. Then another. Another. Dropping babies, another, another (how lovely) on the Normandy Coast.

Sophie thinks the child. The child might have. The child might have pointed to the sky and said starling, larkspur, lark. She writes it down. She takes out her box of paints, thinks: the child. A flock of extinct birds pass. Sophie thinks the child. Against a setting century.

To have had to work for money through the whole pregnancy when all I wanted to do was to sit in my chair with my legs on an ottoman draped in cashmere. Some other time perhaps.

A dream in vivid red last night. Red sky, red sea, red in the toilet bowl. Red falling from my eyes like tears. Fear translating immediately into dream. Yesterday I fell outside my apartment in Providence. Carrying too many papers and books back from school.

A bleeding dream in red.

Then next, the child-gone-from-the-belly dream. And then the dream of the car skidding out of control. A cracked windshield. A crimson wreath in the snow. A bathtub filled with blood-red roses.

Against a terrible and extraordinary music. She takes the child's hand. Make a mountain peak, then cross it. A. *They draw an* A. *And the world begins again.*

I begin to worry a little about the three flights of very narrow stairs up to my garret. Why am I living the life of the graduate student I never was? No telephone. A futon. Bad take-out Chinese food. Stacks and stacks of books.

And Sophie having washed the page in rose (before night) writes Larkspurs (she loved flowers), a book for children.

The fantasy of hurling myself out of this too-small window. The garret stifling. I see us smashed on the street. Not a happy sight.

I still try to write, to work on Frida or *The Bay of Angels* a little, but it is as if I am reaching through haze, through gauze—impossible to get to—to get close enough to. How to get to what matters most? A dying feeling. Of lights being extinguished. Blow out the candles now. It's even getting hard to read. Intimations of the first trimester—enormous fatigue.

She washes the page in spring (where children play).

30 MARCH—29 WEEKS

No getting around the baby anymore. A privacy made completely public.

I look at my notes and see that she is everywhere. Has always been there. Asleep in the text. Rose and baby snow.

She washes the page in rose under the title: Hope.

Welcome to the Children's Museum. Under glass or in a locked box preserved: what they loved, what they wanted, the games they played.

A silver cup, a xylophone, a see-saw, a sliding pond. Three types of seeds—columbine, bluebell, larkspur. A tinker toy. A jump rope. A pink blanket. The rhyming alphabet.

I don't seem like such a complete oddball to the secretaries at Brown anymore. Finally I have something like credibility. Finally we have something huge in common. It's kind of sweet. I could stand there hour after hour suddenly talking babies with them. I savor this being like everyone else for once. Picture myself a normal person, consider what my life might have been like—had absolutely everything been different.

And to the world at large. I am someone suddenly who bears a resemblance to something.

I get many many Normal Person credits for being pregnant, for having a baby. For joining the human race.

For foregoing the husband, for writing all night, for living in my own private Idaho, and for being, in general, a basket case, I get points taken away.

Sophie guides the child's hand. What is this ache deep within for something I do not directly remember, but which was mine?

My writing, as usual, notes to the most mysterious part of myself. Meditating the child—for years and years, before I acted.

Roses and angels, the century, fall on the horizon, and snow. Feel them now as they move slowly into you. They're sweet and round—everything for a while—and you are getting, you are—undeniably—getting sleepy.

The ongoing dream in those years. Roses and apples and snow—the child. Waving and waving on the horizon.

The oddness at the very heart of me.

Once after a reading a bunch of us went to dinner. A friend of Dixie's, the judge, sat down next to me and said, "You know, don't you, that you are a very strange person."

C.D. and I in a Creative Writing faculty meeting. God, she says in her Arkansas accent, *you look just like Rapunzel!* It is true, I don't know why, but I've just let my hair grow and grow. And it's much thicker, more wild than usual.

I named my baby Rapunzel so that she might display ingenuity. So that she might dream of escape.

4 APRIL

The baby takes in the three days of our festival celebrating New Directions. James Laughlin is dead. When I wrote earlier in the year he was pleased by our plans though his health precluded his joining us. Michael Palmer comes, which cheers me greatly. Walter Abish, Robert Creeley. Beloved Rosmarie Waldrop like a New Directions queen. I read from John Hawkes's *The Blood Oranges*. He's decided to sit this one out. I understand. First I say how he and ND changed my life. Then I read—it sounds great out loud. Pregnancy makes you cry at every turn and so I am weeping for the very *fact* of Jack Hawkes. The very *fact* of New Directions. I was late to the dinner because of course I'd lost my keys again. I'm in love with the New Directions editors. They are incredibly smart and serious, the last thing you think of an editor being anymore. It makes me terribly nostalgic, longing for a past in which I might have been a writer in such a situation. Yes, it might have been me, that graceful give and take, finally the perfect match—I am consistently challenged, basking in their guidance, their brilliance, their devotion to the text as we amble along the still bohemian Greenwich Village streets, a past which for me never existed—but which was mine. They advance me enough money to write. Not much, but not much is needed. We are in the last smoke-filled, amber-lit afternoons before publishing completely changes forever. Books will become commodities. So-called serious writers will find the formulas to make themselves famous and rich. Experimental work will be completely scoffed at and ridiculed—but not yet. The young corporate writers of today are not even born yet, I hope. There are still small publishers, not conglomerates, a belief in the possibility of art.

These marvelous editors, talking this afternoon about translation—these women from a disappeared world, back here with us for a second. I rub my eyes. Am I dreaming?

I'd like to do a big book with them.

The music I live and write to all hours of the day that drives everyone crazy. I know from the beginning she has heard it.

Mom tells my sister Christine. She seems all right with it for now. Generous, even kind. Trying so hard always to claim her small bit of happiness. Not giving up. I don't know how she goes on sometimes. I admire her courage.

I wish I could give her some of this peace.

We dare to name her. We feel now as if it is real—or at least more real.

Rose.

To be surrounded on both sides by roses—my mother, and now my daughter. What could be better than that?

Mother. Daughter—
"A rain of roses will fall at my death."
—Saint Therese of Lisieux

Rose
for my mother
and for Gertrude Stein
and for Rosmarie Waldrop too
No other name in the world.
Rose, still enclosed in her translucent amnion. Her heartbeat is louder now.

Every rose pulses.

A very sweet long lunch with Jack Hawkes. A while back I had inadvertently offended him by making a frivolous comment about some of his former students, now writers of some note (I did not even know they were his students). An awkward and painful few weeks. A lot of prima donna posturing from the former students. It all having to do with their posing as experimental avant-garde types at the experimental avant-garde festival while simultaneously reading their slickest work from *The New Yorker,* and flinging their various issues of the magazine around the stage. I am offended and find the way to say so. Pressure from the program for me to apologize. I write a goofy letter trying to *explain myself* to the former students. Imagine! The whole thing is absurd.

But Jack takes the whole thing to heart. Months and months

pass. I try to apologize. He tries to dismiss it. *It was nothing.* How can I tell him what he has meant to me? Of course I can't. And so we talk about other things, happy things. The baby. The book. The film of *The Blood Oranges.* He thinks Rose is a lovely name. There aren't many Roses, really, he says. He thinks Styron. He does a brief critical assessment of William Styron. You can imagine! We eat pasta and I break my no-drinking rule for the afternoon. It begins to rain. When I leave him he disappears down Thayer Street in the fog to buy typewriter ribbon. That spectral genius. Waving good-bye.

The increasing need now for solitude. This turning inward. More even than usual—though I have always craved it. Once on a beach long ago I move my towel away from my chatting friends and declared, I need my solitude. Many years ago now. It came up many times after that as a joke almost: *Give Carole her solitude.*

My students comment on how I am very nearly unrecognizable without a glass of wine in my hand. I guess in this way at least I must be a real old-fashioned writer. AA smugly waits for me. Not a chance.

When she wakens she moves about freely in the buoyant fluid, turning from side to side and frequently head over heels, as it is said of one who is madly in love.

She falls back to sleep. The baby floating in her dreamy amnion.

Saw a documentary on TV and realized I knew the people in it a little. Enough to know it was not going to end well. The film concerned the different aspects of wanting and having a child. A brother and his wife trying to get pregnant. A sister and her lesbian lover and their infant. I brace myself. Right before the baby's first birthday, the sister will be killed by a driver who runs a red light late at night. Unspeakable sorrow. I watch Mary, the sister of the woman killed, the woman I know a little, weeping uncontrollably on the TV screen at the baby's birthday party.

Is there any way at all to be safe?

Helen, held at gunpoint, only months after she'd become sober. Her whole life still ahead of her.

"The amnion, though transparent and hardly thicker than the paper of this book, is tough and slightly elastic, like sausage casing. Unlike sausage casing, it is quite lovely and has a natural silvery shimmer. It is a living tissue made up of a single layer of skin cells."

You are gleaming inside. In your bag of waters. It cushions you now against blows—and keeps you warm—and supports you so that you are virtually weightless. You are covered now in a coat of grease like a channel swimmer. It is called *vernix*—that is Latin for varnish.

And as if that were not enough you grow fuzz—*lanugo*, Latin for wool, on your arms and legs and back. My darling lamb. My lambling.

Earthling now . . . almost.

Another rare occasion where I allow myself a drink (I can count them on one hand). The artist Annette Messager has come to Brown to speak. She is marvelous, of course. Her women's work—without apology. I wave to Sylvie across the aisle. Good French champagne afterwards—impossible to resist. I don't know why a few drinks effect me this way, but they do. When I return to my room I curl up on the floor naked hugging the curvature of my body and weep. I am Mahler's *Lied von der Erde.* I am singing. I am elemental. I am the earth and the sorrow of the earth. In the translation: *Dark is death, is life* . . . I open in concentric circles. *Everywhere and forever the distances shine blue.* I am the blue beauty of the earth. I am eternity. I am radiance. Oh, God! What a sight!

The things I love to do most: writing novels, gardening, cooking, being pregnant—women's work, all.

This little book was meant to chronicle the workings of time on the psyche and the body. And yet now I notice that time seems oddly suspended, hanging there—or even reversed. A bizarre feeling.

7 APRIL

First copy of *Defiance* in my hands. Suddenly I worry I have been too passive during its production. Done too little (nothing in fact) to ease it into the world. To help its reception. It's a very strong piece of work—if it's overlooked this time, well, then someday. It is what I have come to believe.

Try not to second-guess it all. Try to relax a little. I am not a salesman for God's sake. (How old-fashioned I sound). Isn't it hard enough to write them? Of course it is. I do not sell many books, I'm afraid. As if I should. Considering what sells. The crass, the vulgar, the simplistic, the sensational. I despise it. I'll save the lecture I guess. How nice—a little of the old arrogance coming back!

The odd thing about being pregnant—I care even more deeply than before about my writing, but less and less about my writing "career."

But did I neglect it? The question nags a little today. I have scarcely thought about it since that major revision to the galleys. Knew then it was as close to the book I wanted as it would get. And I let it go. Helen asks how I feel about seeing it for the first time, but I don't really know. It's a far-off object, like almost everything.

8 APRIL

Worried now about flying on one big plane and one small plane to Penn State but am quite desperate to try to find a teaching position where I will only have to be there half the year. Something Brown has so far been unwilling to agree to.

Violence of the rise into the sky. Usually I am thrilled by it. But today all I can think is that this is not natural. What am I doing? That awful tilted centrifugal thing. The horizon askew. I feel like the scarecrow in the *Wizard of Oz*—torn in pieces by the velocity, by the height, the pressure in the cabin. The baby protests. What I am doing is trying to save my life. Anything for one semester. But anything?

Why am I all the way up here?

I wish Helen were here to take my hand as we take off.

On the small plane now. Too late I realize it was a mistake to come. Feeling very strange. Strange indigestion. Why did I think this was worth the risk? Have decided I will drive back with Robin instead of flying again. It will be fun to spend time with her.

Ten years ago this spring. Robin was there. I walked the streets of Vence—a complete *folle.* Hanging on to that notebook for dear life. Season of the *Bal des Pompiers, Front National,* the three thieves. Stéphane. Thought if I carried his child I'd be saved.

In last night's dream the way I know I am in premature labor is that everything on the TV is backward and upside down. The frantic search for a TV at Penn State as a result today in order to verify that I am OK. How I hate the specificity of dreams. The exactitude of their demands, their clarity, their obviousness. The way they can convince you that absolutely anything is plausible.

Good Friday. Prayers to Saint Clare.

Interview with *Publishers Weekly. PW* has always been smart about my books and I do not take that for granted. Seemed very interested in this as my first "mainstream" book, and yet it seemed the interviewer wanted to hear very little about what I actually had to say about this. Not sexy enough, I suppose. My mythic hydra-headed self a lot more entertaining, I guess.

12 APRIL, EASTER SUNDAY

The conventionality of children—the hubris of boys—even the sweet ones. Nicholas, my nephew, four years old, as mild a boy as is possible to find, asks, *How did you get the baby?* I tell him the same as everyone gets one. *Then you were married?* I say you don't have to be married to have a baby. No. And he says after thinking about it for a minute, *Get married.* Emily, his sister, the more opinionated and vocal one usually, just listens. Having no comment, but sensing—sensing what? The authority and judgments of little boys—even at age four. Something in the genetic code? Or the socialization process? Or perhaps it is a survival instinct? Little dictators. Even the sweetest of them. Get married, the baby patriarch commands.

On the other hand my seven-year-old niece Katie gleefully announces to her class, *My aunt is having a baby and she didn't even have to get married!* She thinks this is one of the greatest things she's ever heard.

15 APRIL

Finally I've left Providence for the country to sit on my nest full time. It is the waiting now that is beautiful. This handful of days left. The absence of distraction.

In what we imagined paradise, serenity—spring in the country—a tick burrows its way into the back of my leg while I am out gardening.

Louis and Louise in their utmost kindness. They are wondering what helpful thing they can do next. They have prepared me little chickens. They have read me interesting things from magazines until I've drifted off to sleep. Now, Louise has found a gargantuan African dress in her closet for me to put on.

The questions of who am I and why am I here and all the rest give way now to what is a layette, and how long do you boil an egg?

How remote *Defiance* and all that rage seem to me now. It is as if all of a sudden someone in my head has adjusted the controls.

20 APRIL

A robin redbreast sits on her nest in the giant rhododendron outside my bathroom window that was once filled with snow. How intent she looks sitting there. I stand on top of the toilet seat to see the eggs. Three.

Rose in waiting. Rose on the verge.

I love the seasons. How one thing turns into another. It is for me where all hopefulness lies. In the transformations.

The other thing that always kept me from having a baby: I never could imagine a future of any kind—and I do not quite know why. *No future, no future for you.* Johnny Rotten and the Sex Pistols sang my mantra in those years. It was before I began writing in earnest—when I was still completely lost. Could not imagine living. Not until 1986, when Gary died. After that it would take another twelve years to be ready to consider a child. To trust the notion of future. My God! At the pace I move.

Another aspect I notice is the belief in a self a journal necessarily implies. Confirmation of a construction I am not quite sure is real.

An odd time. Who do I concoct in these pages as the protagonist?

The teller of tales—and who do I assume will be interested? Do I write this solely for myself? How disingenuous am I, without knowing it?

Dr. Rehrer, who has not been around much at all, has now dropped out altogether. She has lupus. *New York* magazine has just named her one of the city's best doctors. She laughed cynically. She'll have to close her practice. I will stay with Dr. Matheson. Some say he does not have the bedside manner, but that he is the best. I am over forty. Not interested in bedside manner, hate sympathy, support groups, sharing, reaffirmations, etc. He's my man: black, early middle age, and as calm as can be, *the most natural thing in the world.*

I turn my thoughts toward childbirth now. Begin to read.

> In a flash I see you risen—
> my sore rose Eros—ecstatic
> in the mounting flush, a volcano
> under snow, crowing to greet
> the dawn within you.
>
> —*L. S. Asekoff*

The floating technique.

"The contractions seem to be coming in waves now, so it is valuable to think of relaxing the whole body and letting it float up to the peak of a contraction's strength so you can just slip over the top" (from a Bradley Method pamphlet).

It sounds thrilling in a way and I realize I have waited my whole life for this.

Baby care class at St. Vincent's. As I have not a clue what to do with a baby once a baby is produced. Sitting in a room of pregnant women and their mates. The husbands seem pale, shadowy, ghosts of themselves. Helen's gone up to work on the house, so I am here alone. It's fine with me. I like the space to think my thoughts, to dream. No running commentary necessary. These ordinary women all made extraordinary by their state. The power of eight pregnant women in one room—if we could harness that power it seems we might do anything—cleanse rivers, stop wars, bring on world peace. I notice what a secret this is kept. How belittled pregnant women are by our culture. How taken for granted. It doesn't surprise me.

These women. I forget for a minute that they are really just human. Shocked to hear one of them being catty and insensitive when talking to a couple in the room who is about to adopt. Yet even she somehow mysteriously transcends her own mediocrity—carrying a miracle as she is.

A white room. Eight states of grace.

Despite themselves they radiate mystery, incredible darkness and light. I must say they all seem dull when they speak, but they are doing this miraculous work.

The miracle of us in that room.

In these last weeks I already miss being pregnant. If it could only be like writing a book. I always have one begun before the previous one ends. Protection of sorts. I might have had twenty children. Alas. In another time or life. Am I crazy? Yes, a little, today.

Oh, the might-have-been—that melancholy tense.

My genuine physical aptitude for making and carrying children —the ease in my body, a certain animal trust—I feel a genius of sorts at it. I am happy and well, and without nervousness. Looking forward to the birth. Am I crazy? Probably.

"Think your way up and over this contraction, locating any tension that is left in your body and letting it go, letting it ease through your hands and feet" (Bradley Method). *Think* your way through?

In the doctor's office today a lot of end-of-the-pregnancy people looking genuinely miserable. I am uncomfortable but really quite happy. I love my latest shape. True I am incredibly unwieldy, cannot turn over in bed. I am more like a beached whale than a person these days. Seem to only have beached whale thoughts. But I am happy. I am unfazed by the inability to sleep. I have never been able to sleep.

This will be a happy book.

The article in *PW* comes out, slightly more garish and sensational than one would hope, but all in all, all right. An old jab at Gordon Lish makes its way into the pages. Retrieved from old interviews, I guess. The Knopf-as-a-whorehouse quote—all the greatest hits—the wit and wisdom of C.M. How removed I feel from my former self and from publishing in general. It all seems silly from this vantage point. Only the work matters. Only the baby. Helen. My family. My handful of friends. I am back to the barest and most essential. Film, music, of course. The trees.

God, the trees this time of year in the country! Have they ever been so magnificent?

Exhausted by even the idea of *Defiance* in the bookstores.

Saw my first copy on a front table at B. Dalton today. Thought it looked beautiful. Really much more beautiful than the rest of the books. I pat it on the back. I wish it well. When I open to a random page and read, it still burns in my hand. A good sign, I think.

On Wednesday a book party at Cathy Murphy's gallery, Lennon, Weinberg. Reading is hard with all the breathlessness. Reviews starting to come in. Great or terrible, over-inflated or condescending, they have never much mattered to me. Though some of the mean-spiritedness has hurt me, and some of the stupidity offended me.

The sudden need to finish Frida before the baby comes. My way of feathering the nest, I suppose. God, what kind of mother am I going to be? A bed of words.

For a soon-to-be-born present we get you *Lolita* read by Jeremy Irons on tape. Figuring she might want to hear something good by now.

Feeling very antsy to get to *The Bay of Angels,* but that is always the case when trying to finish up a book. The charge of the new versus the drudgery of the almost-finished. Also there are the essays to get together.

Very, very tired.

Feeling very vulnerable with the arrival of *Defiance* in the world.

Went shopping in my daze for something to wear Wednesday night. Can't get away with any of the regular dresses—even the very largest sizes won't accommodate this belly. No one in real life has a belly quite this big. I find something finally at A Pea in a Pod. Odd to be a pod. And yet that is distinctly the feeling.

Aishah presides over the baby blessing up at the house. Black matriarch—and my mother seated on my right side, white matriarch. Though I dreaded it (the very idea of a shower), still it was a very moving, very lovely event. My mother trying to remember a lullaby her mother once sang her long ago.

Friends not seen for a very long time. What keeps me separate, apart from even those I love?

More notations these days I notice—now that I am free of school.

7 MAY

The book party was fairly painless. Mercifully there was something else to talk about other than the book. The book always over for me by the time it is published. Trying to keep up some enthusiasm always a chore. But tonight there is a new subject. *I am having a baby! Yes, we see!* A surprise to many of the people there.

Back to quiet, after the book party, the baby blessing, the social whirl.

Purple lilacs against a blue field of hills, above it the lighter sky. My gray cat Fauve on my lap. All is still. The baby moving.

Dreamt she was born blind. Anxiety for the first time.

Dinner with Georges and Anne Borchardt. It was very nice to see them. Georges tells a funny story about ordering Anne's dinner for her in the hospital after she delivers their daughter. Such a wonderful French man! I don't see him much, but I revere and respect and in a strange way adore him. Irrationally. It has kept us from really being friends, I'm afraid.

Washington, D.C.—too long a ride just to do a reading. The car feels like a tomb. The book shall take care of itself. I have to stop this.

We all listen to *Lolita* the whole way.

Gordon Lish after all these years still acting like an ass. Saw the *PW* piece and is throwing a little fit.

Oh, for the days of Marimekko muumuus—who said that the other day looking at me?

A radio interview downtown in one of the federal buildings. When I'm done I look up and see a sign that says marriage licenses. We've been meaning to do this for years. I call up Helen and she comes down and we get our domestic partnership certification. Or do they call it a license? Practical reasons motivate me. If we don't do this they could, in the event of Helen's death, take the apartment away from me. She wishes I were more romantic. But I have always distrusted such conventions—the ceremonies and sanctions. The buying into a prefabricated value system. The assumptions. The burdens. It's stifling. It makes it impossible to breathe or live anywhere. We are on line with two women who are going to have an enormous "wedding" that weekend. We hear about the invitations, the parents flying in, the church, the food, the band. They have set up a register at Ikea. Some of my usual condescension returns, some of the old disdain. Astutely they note my condition and I tell them that we've been together for twenty years and that she is finally making an honest woman of me.

The Afghanistani I bought a banana from downtown before my interview rubbed my stomach and said something in his language. What are you saying, I ask him?

I am praying for a boy.

Worries all of a sudden pile up. All that lead paint in our country house. And what about that antibiotic cream? Can't sleep.

Dreams of the blind baby. Sunglasses and a little cane.

The baby's nursery hardly begun. And the bathroom in the middle of renovation. Because the old bathroom is no place for a baby. Too much mess and chaos, however. Renovating in late pregnancy. Why have we waited until the last minute? I can't live like this. Wake up with a hundred lists in my head.

bassinet
crib
bouncy seat
layette

Want only my solitude. To fall into the silence with you.

What is a layette?

15 MAY

How far off these days *The Bay of Angels* seems. My coveted time off from school, the beginning of my obscurity finally arrived—or so I had hoped. After three years at Brown in "show time" mode—a kind of party hostess/workhorse. One crisis, one festival, one dean or another every time I turned around. How much I have craved my solitude, my time alone. The book, after a lifetime of preparation, finally ready to be written. The time presenting itself at last. What am I doing? What have I done? One month until the baby.

Dr. Matheson suggests I think about staying a little closer to the hospital now. So here I sit in the apartment, quasi-hysterical over the color of the walls. I can't be in early labor in this color! And Helen, on top of everything else she is doing, begins to paint. And I can't breathe with all these books. And let's get a TV so I can rent movies—it's no longer possible to read. I spend most of the day now just walking around. Visiting the doctor. On some weekends I still go to the country. As Dr. M. says, as long as you are only two hours away. *The baby is not just going to pop out.* That's a good thing, I think.

New York is really the perfect place for these last weeks. I welcome New Yorkers' indifferent attitude (seen that, been there) with relief. The hostility of some youngish women (Oh, God, I forgot to have a baby) now going completely by me. I *am* having one. There is nothing I can do about it. There is no room for anything else in my head.

Also the problem of having to cook anymore disappears here. Anything you want is already made. I carry a little vodka tomato sauce from Home Away From Home, toddling down Bleecker Street. Rented another armful of movies.

Less room in there for kicking and moving around. It's getting pretty crowded, I guess. I read at an uptown Barnes and Noble.

Have dinner with Dixie and her friend Barbara. Do you want it to be over? I am fairly surprised by my answer. *No.*

Memorize this. For you will never feel or look this way again. You will never. There is a marked sadness about such a definitive statement now.

Dwindling last days.

Irrational last days. All the past months of serenity giving way to a kind of mania. Finishing the house, childbirth classes, things to buy: diapers, sleeping wedges—Oh, God. Impossible to focus.

Nietzsche: One must still have chaos in oneself to be able to give birth to a dancing star.

Oh God, I know I'm far gone when I start quoting Nietzsche.

Impatience today at being so unwieldy, and yet reluctance, even in this humidity, to let go of being pregnant. Having given over my body so completely at this point.

To be inhabited by an angel. How often does that happen?

An angel in residence.

Only weeks (days?) away from my life never being the same again. And after forty-plus years one is used to one's life. Why this coincides with the chance to write *The Bay of Angels* I do not know, do not even pretend to comprehend. It haunts me. I cannot let go of it.

The gaze far off—a little sorrowful—carrying this mortal creature inside.

Something ending in me.

Pesticides, plastics, PCPs, dioxin in the breast milk in Japan, tears in the ozone, forests dying—I hand you this ruined planet —to cherish.

I get my lead level checked. What if I am poisoning her, living in that old house? All the renovation we've done in the last five years suddenly terrifies me.

Feelings that the baby has died. Every kind of nightmare.

Dr. M. says that she is in ready position.

Her head on my bladder.
The bones in the pubis opening like a butterfly.
The bones of the hips unhinging.
The ribs floating open like water.
All this to allow the child through.

More and more I long to swim.

A beautiful day in New York. I can see that. But everything is so far away. I feel so removed, as in the very beginning. This preparation for life. This rehearsal for death. Can't touch, can't reach anything anymore. Doesn't everyone look busy out there going about their business—reading the newspaper and rushing to the subway and thinking about what they will do this weekend.

I open *The Bay of Angels.*

Her feet at my heart.

Lead level comes back a minuscule 2.2 in my blood.

Dixie cooks us dinner. We see her once a week now. A great treat. And Ilene. I have lunch with her on Mondays and wait. A reunion—after all we've been through. This baby girl brings us back together. It's one of the miracles of this time.

The mortal body—one cannot help but feel it. Carrying two deaths inside me now. I am responsible. I am indicted.

Laura sends Stein's *The World Is Round*—starring Rose. Rosmarie sends a tiny baby-sized edition. One of my very favorites.

I am two whole people now. How to describe the strangeness?

Such mildness and surrender. The book out there. More

reviews. Excessive praise means little. Being slighted makes no difference.

Are you afraid of giving birth? This answer less surprising. *No.*

Everyone else more nervous now than I am now. They all seem to be hurrying around me. I, motionless at the center. After a brief flurry of hysteria I am back in my Buddha zone.

The fact is by the time a book is published I have no stake in it at all—my writing life is elsewhere. This angle of mind has served me well. Afforded me a kind of useful distance. Odd to be interviewed though—can't remember a thing really. How did you write it, what were your intentions—the usual questions.

The fact is no work of mine once it is published interests me in the least.

27 MAY

Helen's six-year sober anniversary—without which there would be no house, no Coco, no Rose, no Carole—we count on our fingers at dinner, astonished.

Schneiders, 20 Avenue A—in the heat, in my blur, we look at carriages, cribs, the famous layettes.

28 MAY

The baby begins her graceful descent, undeniably.
Mozart's floating line of sixteenth notes . . .

You need a great patience at the end.

"My patience is of wood, mute, vegetative."
—*Caesar Vallejo*

No, there are no more somersaults now. She's outgrowing her house of blood and light.

baby bonnet
pacifier
bibs

A long conversation in the rain with my friend Louis. I don't want our friendship ever to change. I want it to remain exactly like this and forever. But with the baby—I worry I shall lose him in some way. God, can I find anything else to worry about?

The baby descends. Her head engaged in the tight-fitting circle of pelvic bones like a crown. I'd like to follow her dream down but I think I'd better make some arrangements for childbirth classes fast. The last time we tried to go, a Saturday, all day—seven earnest couples—the instructor failed to show. It felt like a reprieve somehow. Difficult to explain.

Suddenly I am panicked. What if I have the baby before the classes? Dr. M. looks at me bemused.

White people.

Private childbirth sessions at Soho Pediatric with Michelle Simon, who is wonderful. I will be a Bradley Method girl, more or less. Bradley, the *other* natural childbirth method. I hear you just act like you're sleeping. Sounds OK. I can't bear the idea of all that panting the Lamaze people do. Makes me dizzy just to think of it.

Lots to prepare for and learn. Helen seems nervous. I am alarmingly serene. Even when we go through what will happen in the last stage of labor—Michelle holds up a large poster showing impossibly jagged lines meant to denote pain. Lovely early rounded hills turns into Appalachian peaks. She walks us through all the various scenarios. This might happen, or this. *Not that.* Yes. We amble over to St. Vincent's to see the set-up. Wept when I saw the Pitocin machine, the contraption that dispenses a medication to induce labor, because it looked enough like the I-Med, that thing Gary was on. These halls. The Coleman Wing. I'm in the same place he was. What shall be the proximity of our rooms?

Michelle says I will not be feeling like wearing my lipstick in the third stage of labor, but I find this rather unlikely.

Everyone has been born after all. How hard can it be?

Mystery of book and rose. Rose and baby snow.

Not one real drop of blood in all these nine months. I wonder about the effect of seeing it again after all this time. The violence of it, its vibration and hum. Always incredibly attuned to color. Thought I might be a painter. No such luck. Insistence, loss, finality. Ruby flame, the grand finale. The shock of blood. Blood after no blood.

I feel in some actual emotional danger. Like I've gone too far. Like I've relied on a faulty sense of confidence and peace. Impossible to describe. On insanity's verge tonight.

What was I thinking? To create a being who is going to suffer. To be responsible, utterly, for someone's death. A grave indictment. It was not a lark. Did I take this all too lightly? How else was I to take it and still go forward?

I sit expectant in the big city, waiting. Helen up at the house with Angela. They've been moving in the bathtub. When the phone rings, she tells me later she hopes it is not me in labor because they haven't eaten their veal chops—still on the grill—brought up from Balducci's.

Is there a floor yet in the bathroom? I want to know. I need a floor.

I have many things to buy in the pharmacy for my impending labor. I waddle over there. It's a weird list.

plastic shoes for the shower
a scarf? for my head? (It's supposed to help you concentrate)
tennis balls?

lollipops
candles
massage oil
lip balm

I have in my head that I will also need the Schubert *Impromptus*, but I keep forgetting to get them.

Doubt very much I am going to wear a scarf around my head during labor. The last thing I want is to look like David Foster Wallace.

About a home movie made right before his birth, from Nabokov's *Speak Memory:*

> He saw a world that was practically unchanged—the same house—the same people—and then realized that he did not exist there at all and that nobody mourned his absence. He caught a glimpse of his mother waving from an upstairs window, and that unfamiliar gesture disturbed him, as if it were some mysterious farewell. But what particularly frightened him was the sight of a brand-new baby carriage standing there on the porch, with the smug, encroaching air of a coffin.

People who have vaguely despised me for having something they did not: love, talent, confidence. Now their rage, undisguised. *Who do you think you are?*

I rent three films at a time now from Evergreen. Have a list of really mindless ones (any Hollywood movie) for when early labor begins. Something meant to be vaguely amusing, but not too demanding, as the event begins.

1 JUNE

Ambivalence, obviously, at the end.

Yes, but can one imagine completely forgoing a major life experience? Yes. Today, yes.

Once there was almost a child with apple cheeks conceived in snow and she was called Rose. Apples and roses and snow. Angels at our feet. Mercy.

Almost a child, I had written in 1993. Angel. What did I know? Uneasiness at the end. Not to see portent in everything. Especially not in this.

Are you afraid? The question surprises me every time. I am many things, but I am not that. It has never occurred to me to be afraid. Afraid of what?

I sing her an old Kinks song all day long: *So tired, tired of waiting, tired of waiting for you.*

I've got my hot rice sack to use during labor. They'll microwave it right up at St. Vincent's, Michelle chirps. And afterwards for those tender breasts—bags of frozen peas!

Take out almost every night now from Home Away From Home on Bleecker Street. Carrying my little container of vodka and tomato sauce. Can't be bothered to think of what else to eat. Find the old urge to drink beginning to return. The vodka tomato is as close as I get though.

The physicality of pregnancy—a most exhilarating thing. I am grateful, have been grateful, for all of it.

Plush, lush, luscious. Flushed with blood and beating life. Oh!

This lovely trusting little passenger.

We orbit one another. I, her—or she, me. Hard to tell anymore. This universal music. This feeling more and more each hour of being on the verge of some impending revelation.

A bizarre suspended life in the weeks just before the baby. Time hanging in abeyance. An odd concentration moves in. Also weird lapses in memory, time. Little sleep now. It's too hard to find a good position. I use three pillows. Also walking in the city streets a bit more challenging. They're uneven as always and my bones are all wavy now. My little collapsible ankles. My body opening up like a door, like a rose.

My life in abeyance. My life, two lives.

Rose, on the very verge.

I hear Grieg's *Cradle Song* and weep.

We are two souls in one body. I am holding two souls. Moving and not moving through time and space.

2 JUNE

They are fixing the steps in front of Our Lady of Pompeii in the heat and I am in one instant back in Italy.

The Cafe Milou, new on Seventh Avenue, in one moment takes me back to France. Intense heat. And then suddenly I am in Greece. How many places have I wandered through alone? Loving that feeling. I am never to be singular again. Always double—wherever I walk in the world.

Even if I were to go somewhere without her, already it is clear, she will always be there by my side. Perhaps the reason most people have children in the first place—and the reason I almost did not.

Haunted all winter by a shadow next to my shadow as I walked down the path in the country to the car. Three-year-old Rose there at my side. I never see her; I see only her shadow next to my shadow—in winter.

3 JUNE

Feeling a bit odd, altered statey somewhat. Just different than before. Also a bit nauseous, crampy—all the classic signs?

Still trying to finish up Frida. It's probably hopeless. Why can't I, even now, entirely give in?

You are in the garden of an inn on the outskirts of Prague.
You feel completely happy a rose is on the table
And instead of writing your story in prose you watch
The rosebug which is sleeping in the heart of the rose.

—*Apollonaire*

Defiance: I have taken a certain kind of narrative as far as it will go. I can go no farther with it. I've done that now for good. What a relief. Just another way now to be free.

Calm beyond all reason. A day in the country. Doing a bit of gardening. Feeling as if Rose is right here with me. It's as if she is inside and outside at the same time. I tell her about the flowers. She's right here.

It is at the edge of a
petal that love waits.

—*W. C. Williams*

A great concentration and focus moves in. Not unlike the feeling when really writing. But there is no really writing anymore.

A reading from *Defiance* at Barnes and Noble. *Defiance* an unusual project for me. Enacting as it does a pain so intense and insistent that it opens up onto something else entirely in the end. Something close to radiance. Is it the accretion? How is the effect achieved? Mysterious to me still.

Weekend (if I make it)
Enter final changes to Frida.

Reread and reorder pieces.
Print out at Louis's house.
In handwriting enter Dear Cathy pieces and see if they work at all.

Read again.

Include in Frida or no? A series of meditations in the form of letters to my friend, the painter Cathy Murphy, written as part of the Frida études.

August 1995
Dear Cathy,

A strange recurring daydream—my life in front of me in some sort of visual representation—difficult to explain—there it was before me—an abstract shape—a precious, shimmering thing—and how afraid I was to waste it—in bravado, in drama, a hundred utterly compelling and senseless affairs—which somehow made sense, and yet—

I am pulled in too many directions. Children. To worry it now seems silly. Frida with her fetus in a bottle. Her ardent desire for a child. I am not really like her—my monstrous ambivalence. Helen says we shall be lonely one day. But my fear of having to work my whole life for money. To never get close to the book I know I must write. The vague feeling of this somewhere in some distance.

Do you think of this ever?

A week of teaching in Provincetown. Roses do grow like oceans here. The students so earnest. In the fog horn at night, the births and deaths of angels. I can scarcely sleep. Frida. The way Frida comes and goes. Drawn to the swirling . . . Love to you, dear friend,

C.

The French waitress at Cafe Milou asking, *Would you like strawberries?* To bring on labor, she tells me. And also a celebration, *non*?

Do you like butter? My mother smiles, passing a buttercup under my chin.

A string of beautiful cool June days. It feels like grace.

Ilene calls.

It's June 10th, the day I always predicted the baby would come. A full moon. Helen calls all day long.

Rented Angelopoulos's *Ulysses*. Haven't seen it in quite some time. Also a documentary on Gertrude Stein. There she is playing with Basket and waving to the camera for a second.

Defiance—formally conceived as wave after wave of pain. A series of intensities. Do I, in my own way, prepare for childbirth with these meditations?

June 10th comes and goes. No baby yet. Officially due on the 15th. A letter from Amy T. suggests the 21st would be a great, joyous, planetary-aligned-type day to be born. We shall see.

The uses of a journal: to have a record of the person I was before she ever existed. In this minute the baby is still unborn, and I am still the person who has never experienced childbirth, and who has never even for one day known her yet. The person I once sounded like—before everything changed irrevocably and forever.

Helen and I indulging in all sorts of magic and rituals—a Peking duck last night, that lucky and happy meal—to welcome the baby. Very spicy eggplant. So where is she? I grow less and more patient. Not sure exactly what I want.

Got myself out in the heat to a few shows in Soho. Felt like a farewell of sorts. For who knew when I would see art ever again? A last glimpse—at the New Museum, Doris Salcedo, her table made of wood, cloth, and human hair—at Sperone Westwater, Wolfgang Laib's sculptures of pollen. Robert Irwin's spheres of light . . .

Roaming around Bloomingdale's for things we think we must need. A fan. We pick it up, put it back down again, can't decide on a thing. Very, very distracted. Turning and turning in circles again like a cat.

Ilene and I daydreaming how the baby sucks its house away after its birth. The uterus shrinking. Well worth including somewhere in *The Bay of Angels*—should I ever get there.

This darling child, never one day of trouble—not even one—it seems hard to believe. Maybe she is waiting for Frida to be finished before arriving.

A spate of the most beautiful days on earth.

A flush, a flood of roses. Rose blush. Helen says the garden in the country is filled with roses. *Bring them to me!*

> Come to me.
> O Rose to be.
> Rose light
> Only roses.
> Everything's coming up roses.
> And rain. And I wait.

As if Rose were already out there in the garden with me.

I see you and I whisper to you as a three-year-old by my side: Rose.

Rose in waiting.

A storm of roses.

Will you come then a year from the day Helen prayed so fervently for you over the relics of Saint Clare? She does fast work, that Clare.

Will you come on Bloomsday?

There is a rose by my head while I sleep (out on the fire escape).

Coco and Fauve hanging around a lot now. What do they sense in their animal perfection?

Rented an early Bergman film last night. A real beauty. It took place during the war. Liv Ullman impossibly young. Finished in a crescendo of burning roses: that small, inconspicuous monologue at the end.

The feeling is one of someone who has finally reached the sea. I wake up this morning feeling great relief.

This gorgeous floating paradise.

15 JUNE, MONDAY—THE DUE DATE!

On a chance visit to Dr. Matheson, I am just feeling a little weird—no way to explain it really. He decides to check the baby on the fetal monitor. It's morning. He comes and goes in his usual casual way—*the most natural thing in the world*—but when he looks at the tape he seems for the first time a little concerned. He says softly that the baby is "not responsive," and that I need to go immediately to Saint Vincent's for a sonogram. Count, by the way, on staying, he says.

This child who has never given me even one day of worry. I balk at the news.

A most awful man does the sonogram. Refusing to answer our questions, just staring at the screen, telling us nothing except the baby does not seem to be moving. I drink orange juice to try to get a reaction from her. I move from side to side. He does not speak but in a murmur, and when Helen begs him to repeat himself, he does not. I hate him. Have you felt the baby move in the last few days? I wrack my brains. Yes. When? Yes, I am sure. But not today.

What we learn finally through Dr. M. and Carodean, the maternity nurse, is that there was no respiration, no muscle tone, no movement (they say it flatly, matter of factly) on the sonogram. In this place of healthy babies and faith. The pregnancy must be induced, the baby possibly in trouble. I am shocked. I have not suspected a single thing wrong. Have felt only supreme well-being. Think of my little sister again, about to die on a day I was happy and thought nothing could go wrong. I am calm and hysterical at the same time. I still know she is charmed and all is all right, but the news jars and grates so severely against what I know is true that it makes me doubt everything—every instinct, every hope, every trust.

Dr. M. tries to reassure. Says we will watch for any distress. He explains that some babies simply cannot bear the stress of being born. I will be hooked up to the fetal monitor for the entire labor. I must trust him. There are few options. A C-section can be done if absolutely necessary—and if it will be better for the baby I am ready to have it done right now—but Dr. M. is reserved. We will watch. We will wait and see.

Later we will learn that she scored a four of a possible ten points on her biophysical profile and that this indicated she may not be able to withstand the trauma of labor. All of a sudden we are in the middle of this thing. I must check into the hospital and labor must be induced. I have Helen ask every person we see what the four might mean: the man who mops the floor, the man who rents the TVs, every nurse, every intern. *Oh, for God's sake,* she says. She is acting casual in that way that makes me know she is very, very nervous.

no movement
no tone
no respiration

Cervadil to ripen the cervix—it is applied Monday at noon and it starts to act just before midnight. Another interval of just waiting. In the interim I put on my hospital gown—the gown Gary wore while he was dying. I visit with my parents who have come to offer some moral support (I do not tell them about the four), wait for Helen to come with all the props: CD player, fans, lollipops, three kinds of lip balm, plastic slippers for the shower. There will be no labor in the shower—I am on the monitor all the time. It prints out its news—there's the baby's heartbeat. Weird to be scribbling in this book right now. I cannot believe something might be really wrong. This perfect child. I cannot think it.

Cervix in Latin is neck.

This life preserver of words.

Cervadil sometimes causes labor to start.

Carodean, my nurse—she must have been named for her parents.

I can't keep this record up anymore, though. I need now simply to concentrate.

A night of medium contractions, apparently. It hurts, but not like crazy. Helen sleeps. I let her. I watch the fetal monitor as the night progresses and the pain steadily grows. The baby seems to be doing OK, Dr. Matheson says, but "not great." The fear and sorrow—the strangeness of all this—the pain in comparison feels small, though it grows. One line monitors her heart, the other my contractions. I will watch the contraction graphs through the whole labor. The lines are mild for a long time and then later begin to spell greater things. I see in the curves the hills of southern France. Or sometimes the rounded mountains of the Catskills—my view from a house I once loved. Still love. Time collapsed now. That is later though. This is all being told afterward now, recalled here, as I could not, did not want to write through this. I just wanted to be there. Attentive to all that was happening. Later on the graph I would see Mont St. Victoire. And then I left this world.

She gallops. In the early Germanic languages Rose meant horse. Rose Chloe: Horse, blooming. A star on her forehead. Her galloping heart hooked up all the time to the fetal monitor. Don't go anywhere except to the bathroom, they tell me. And where do you think you're going? they say when I take us off for a little trot. Put your belt back on. The belt that monitors heartbeat and contractions. I promise you we will be free again.

Her tiny heart tapping, tapping.

Helen is upset I can tell but remains strong and relatively calm. Her nervousness manifests itself in the desire for ice cream at 3 A.M., which I will not let her go get, and her inability through the night to stay awake. Sleep always her means of escape. I let her sleep through some of it—sitting up in a chair in room eight on the ninth floor of Saint Vincent's—the labor and delivery wing. Waves of pain—I ride them into day. There's not much moving around as I must stay hooked up. None of the intricate ways of making it through labor, taking showers, sitting on medicine balls and the like, that we practiced. The hope is that the Cervadil will do the trick and I will not have to go on to the Pitocin, or Pit as they call it, or Pit Bull as I will come to know it. A ferocious thing. The hope is that it will not be necessary—though I'm not sure anyone really believes this but me. In the morning, sometime around six, they come looking for a vein for an IV to hydrate me—*that's sounds nice,* but no vein will hold. Checking the so-called vital signs again and again.

Temperature, blood pressure. For nine months my blood pressure has maintained a cool 100 over 70. Four times now the veins collapse. Time to call for the needle man. I play piano music the whole time on my CD player. The human voice too shrill to listen to.

Finally the magic fingers of the anesthesiologist arrive to put in the water IV and I am afloat. Dr. M. arrives shortly after and announces I am two centimeters dilated and 80 percent effaced. Two centimeters is not a whole lot—we need ten to be born. I will have to have the Pitocin. The baby must come out. I am vaguely troubled by his tone, but I am protected now, filled with fluid, completely high on what is about to happen, on the edge of something clearly so amazing. Such portent, such anticipation, as I have never felt. I feel ready for anything.

At 8 A.M. the Pitocin is introduced. Before that Carodean, my great nurse who thank God is back after being away all night, tells me I should take this time to *beautify a little.* Wash up, brush my teeth and hair, whatever I like. I don't like the sound of it. I remember this now from the childbirth classes This is the "collecting yourself" moment before the Pitocin begins to kick in. Time to, as they say, "regroup." It's going to be a bumpy ride. Somehow they are able to convey this to me without saying it straight out. Good luck. Are you ready? I am ready.

9 A.M.: My water breaks. This is one of the most moving and difficult moments of all for me. And I would like to scoop that pale oval as it falls now finally to the floor.

One would like at the last moment to go backwards, back to Rose in waiting, Rose not yet, Rose in hope.

My water breaks and I am heartbroken.

The little girl keening toward and away from home. Or away from one home and toward another—utterly unknown. *Come to me.* And I—am I out here or in there? *Come to me.* But where am I?

Vocalese—a song without words—only vowels, moans, and cries, and much sighing and begging—but not in words—no words for this. At last, to be at last, at the center of that speechless place. To have waited this long—my whole life—to get here.

So disorienting, so harrowing, an entirely new place is not only glimpsed, but actually seen. One is entirely reoriented—realigned—and allowed into a place that has been completely unavailable until now, utterly off-limits. Outside imaginative access. Opened up onto extraordinary mortal suffering never experienced by me before. I change from one kind of person into another. I enter, for what else is there? I step into it—a place of utter remove and estrangement. A reserved place. A place apart. I bite down. Utter house of pain. Populated by a cast of about three or four. No thought here, no words. At the worst, all, everything disappears—I look up onto a place separated by intense waves of heat and cold, blaring light, sound unlike any other. Helen, disappeared, but I know she's there. When I can still comprehend, understand *I* and *there.*

Words fail, even more than usual.

And the two black angels, coming and going—Dr. Matheson and his accomplice—kind and terrible—adjusting the adjusters, at the controls—she keeps cranking it up I know—from the gloating, glaring center of it I can tell. I throw up, twice, three times—she cranks it up more—adjusts it again—I see Helen's eyes slide over to the gauge. Carodean, angel at the adjuster—and my pain adjusts her—lovely, ghostly vision in white, calling from a remote place, *It will be all right.* So much pain and so much beauty. I try to ride it. I try to go to the center of it—meet it at the eye—but I'm no match. Look, I'm no match for it.

Intensity of the waves and I give in—for the first time in my life, perhaps—surrender like never before—in a life marked by what I thought once were surrenders, swoonings, descents. I enter its blackest, most deep center. I no longer think body or pain or baby—I am just there inside the center of my unbearable, mortal life. Where musical notes, little tiny musical notes seem to be playing—divorced from their song—out of context—and the bones of my dead. And the elements. Star, moon, sun. I am hallucinating. I must be delirious. Dark wind in the room. I look up through a veil of thorns and ghosts and disconnected speech. Helen is there and it seems she is shouting something. Shadows in the hall. I go back down.

And how I stare into where I am going, unblinking, exiting into pain—into the pure, ecstatic non-return. Stranger in a strange, secluded place. Wholly interior now. A place so bizarrely intense, so over the edge that to recreate it again—to get back there is impossible—to that place of pure and perfect and extraordinary hell.

I dilate from two to ten centimeters in four hours. I am hearing from somewhere now, *great job.* Music I can't hear exactly on the whole time. The push toward light. Now on a table I am instructed to push, finally to push. I felt no longer acted upon, ambushed, but able finally to act, to do something—a moment of intense exhilaration. The urge to push had grown to an almost unbearable level. And yet to push too soon—the results, they assured me, could be disastrous. So I waited, but I am thrilled when I finally get to actually do something, exhilarated—like I'm actually going somewhere. To the next circle. Such divine transport. The baby wanting, wanting, in its raw need, to live now—to be born. Almost there. I am best at this part. I am rhythmic, I am contracting like wild, and I am pushing, and can I say it now—I am back, and I am loving this high now, every fiber of my being focused on the task, and I feel for the first time in my life, eternity. This opening and opening. Here comes the head. This incredible burning—like a billion suns passing through me. The moment before she breaks through. And I freeze it for a moment, before the next contraction comes—something so momentous, so impossibly, impossibly beautiful. That precious head begins to show. Someone is saying this. The antenna placed on it to monitor the heartbeat is taken off. The whole world there hovering. Carodean coaching not to waste the contraction's pain—but to push—something so exhilarating, so close to a fearful eternity—the shock of the body opening and opening and opening onto forever—onto and past pain, past the waves and up and beyond everything one ever knew. Blasted with light. Vague waves of pleasure pass through me. Smashed into smithereens, I am a thousand shards. And the baby cries. And you feel as if you have or must have blacked out. What the body alone is capable of—the most extraordinary state. My eyes are shut. I feel a sucking now. The baby is at my breast. I can scarcely, scarcely . . .

A transforming, transfiguring thing. Walking into all pain and hope. Most grave and radiant day of my life. The room lit from within by roses.

TV cameras. Someone in a moment's time asking crazy questions about a baby born that day on the Internet. I am apparently an example of a normal person having a normal birth at the same time the little cyborg is born. I start rattling off—God knows what. A low croaky voice comes out of me as I talk about the American penchant for spectacle—that sort of thing. They look at me mystified. Most surreal place. I am holding my baby. I am saying things in the delivery room to the camera. My sister Cathy will see the baby on TV, before she sees her in person. Angela arrives a few moments later, but I do not recognize her at first. Everything altered. I am not really back yet. I call my mother. Remember the words I say exactly: *Rose is born.*

16 JUNE, 12:48 P.M., BLOOMSDAY

Rose is born.

That incredibly odd moment between not being pregnant anymore but not yet really being a mother either. Or not being pregnant, but still feeling pregnant sort of—only there is a baby somewhere too. Where did the baby go?

Carodean wheels me down the long hall and I realize I have never been in a wheelchair before. The nurses and doctors congratulating me on my work. Why are they saying that I remember thinking. What had really happened? Where is Helen? Great through this. Our bond strengthened once more. We have done this thing. Come through it somehow.

The beautiful umbilicus. That sturdy, gorgeous rope from me to you—how it attaches me to worlds—*worlds*—and to time, my mother's mother's mother's mother. It does boggle the mind.

That stubborn, extraordinary cord—what connects me to you forever.

The placenta with its little hood plopped into a plastic pail. Her little home of blood and veins and minerals and blue and gray.

It fades and then is gone—dark angel manipulating a pump, those increasingly large doses of hell. I don't know how much more I can take of this, I say to her. This is her cue to see how I've dilated. Ten. You are ready.

Now you can push.

Now you can hold your breath.

Now you make no noise. It's an entirely different thing all of a sudden.

Watch my facial muscles. When you push you should look like this.

Use the contraction's pain to push the baby through.

Rupturing, breaking apart universe. Helen holding my hand.

At the last minute Carodean goes to get the doctor—it is happening faster than any of us could have imagined now—and for a moment it is just Helen and I alone in the room. An odd feeling. Austerity of the two of us at this precipice. The baby's head peaking through. Just a guess but I don't think she is up to delivering a baby now. It's a strange moment. Like Helen, I and the pain are the only things left in this whole world. Two about to become three.

But then they are back.

The baby's head appearing.

Do you want to see?

No.

A million suns.

Brilliance beyond description.

Sensation.

After the baby's head is out—a curtain of blood—a collar of blood, fountain of blood.

I only hear about it later.

I am trying to see it now in my mind's eye. What it must have looked like.

The wrenching of the self from the self. A solitude like no other.

I hear the doctor say the cord is around her neck. I realize I have given him all of my trust. I have been reliant on his judgments entirely.

Around her neck—but not tightly—around her neck like a necklace they tell me later. From the contraction graph, they knew this in advance.

I hear the doctor saying a great job.

He holds her up to me.

She is a squirmy, slippery thing.

She has a beautiful voice I think.

I close my eyes, and when I open them, *what is that?* I remember thinking exasperated—she is sucking, sucking on my breast. A little expert already. OK, OK.

And how I want to do it all over again. Perversely. Almost immediately. Replay the scene again and again. Never felt such extremity. Such life. Such rigor and recklessness.

She gets a nine out of ten on her very first test—in this world of tests. A point off for little blue hands and feet. If I could have somehow kept her safe and inside, away from the measurements and tests and assessments of this world.

Soon Angela appears, but I don't recognize her at first. She has come from a far place to be here. And so have I.

The nurses saying great job. Maybe it is because I am old. The TV crew. The long hallway to the next room of this world. This life. The continual surprise of it.

The end of a time.

Mourning the end of one thing and the beginning of another. Pulled inexorably down the long hall into the future. Dark thrill of the unknown.

If one could scoop that pale oval from the hospital floor.

I am struck really by how lovely she is. I was expecting a red faced, wrinkly, pointy-headed thing. She is none of this. She is simply gorgeous. A real glamour girl. Long, elegant fingers. A little pouty mouth. *This one is a cutie,* all the nurses say, and *what a beauty!*

A perfectly round head.

The city behind my eyes—the place mortality opened, and you saw it for an instant fully. Actually saw it. You were on the leisurely way there—living your life—but then suddenly there is a brief look given, you are right close up to it. And then no, not yet, it's not quite time—and you are ushered back, only you are holding a child in your arms. There's still work to do.

It's enough to be on the way. If I accomplish nothing else in my life. Just this is miraculous. That I plowed without illusion toward death. Even as I gave life.

And how you stare with your supernatural powers, which have not yet left, but which are wearing off quickly you can already tell—*stay, don't go* . . . I write against its fading now.

The rose at the end of the mind.

The rose burning in the dark of that June afternoon.

The rose at the end of that white corridor. Who waits.

The rose of pain fading—and another rose taking its place.

One leaves that other world reluctantly at first, and then definitively. And there is nothing you can do.

Rien à faire, as Judith and Zenka loved to say. And it is true.

The connection through pain with all the women who are alive—who have ever been alive.

On to a whole new perceptual plane. Close to death, and the violence of life, the beauty and harshness of it. The wrenching of one being from another. The bitterness, the saltiness, something so elemental.

Her voyage toward knowing and back again, begins. "Now that you know all the letters and I have almost forgotten them," Michael Palmer writes in that beautiful poem to Sarah, his daughter.

The fontanels—little fountains. The head pulsing its blood message.

The bones of the head open—they will slowly suture themselves closed.

It's chilly. Ninety-eight degrees in the womb—and now—

How hard it must be to take in breath on one's own. And the heart—on it's own, now.

The baby is perfectly fine, after all the worry. Through all those tests, she must have been sleeping.

The umbilical cord is cut, leaving that healed scar behind eventually—the navel. I can hardly fathom the strangeness.

Carole, exhausted, in a quoting mood. The baby asleep. What an astonishing sentence: the baby asleep.

Yves Simon:

> Whence comes this nostalgia which we carry within us, the kind that makes us sometimes feel that we have lost an immensity?
>
> There are, in these mysterious surges toward infinite spaces and our conception of them, the signs of an attempt to rediscover an immensity of which we were perhaps aware at a given moment, precisely when, at another moment, that awareness has disappeared.
>
> Does each child that comes into the world see itself deprived of an immensity available to it before it was born, well before it had a brain and a consciousness, and which it was able to exploit without any location or landmark, here and everywhere freely?
>
> Life might be the making of a cocoon which isolates from the world a fragment of infinity...

What streams away now? Vortex of stars, universe, the sucking away of everything (and the baby now sucking away her home). The uterus shrinking away. Good-bye.

Put on her belly she swims. On her feet, she does little stepping motions—*don't go—not yet.* Stay a little.

The pigments of her eyes and her skin shift and shift again. The unstable, still-fluid self. All is possibility. All is beauty.

A strange empty feeling. I never knew I was a shell before. I never knew I was a pod. How will I live?

The baby crying.
Dread of the day.
Dread of the night.

Two take away one. To love somehow the take-away. To not see in her what has been taken away, but what has been given.

The placenta, that little hooded house that nourished her, now asleep in a plastic pail.

Embryo—from the Greek, to swell or teem within. I am still there—part of me is still there. My heart swelling. The world. Promise of the little girl.

Considerable loneliness—how odd in the end to have only one body.

"For she was a child, throwing bread to the ducks, between her parents who stood by the lake, holding her life in her arms which, as she neared them grew larger and larger in her arms, until it became a whole life, which she put down by them and said, 'This is what I have made of it! This!'" —*Virginia Woolf*

One and only one life.

She clutches the breast with her million years of monkey intuition. Holding my fur.

This little being asleep in her little hospital cap. In her see-through bassinet.

My father bought for you on day two *Mozart for Babies.*

I'll start a baby book soon. For remembrance. Baby and book—the two most beautiful words in the language.

Baby and book. I write these words now. And the world opens.

This little being asleep before me now.

Breast feeding. Frozen bags of peas on my very sore breasts. Waiting for the real milk to kick in.

The little one holds her cup of witch's milk and weeps.

Overwhelmed by mortality—by the mortal, fragile, tenacious life in front of me. Jemima Puddle-Duck in the form of a cloth rattle near her little chest—going up and down on her baby's breath.

Her lungs the size of tea bags.

I love it high up above the city like this. A preemie flies by. Women in different stages of the dream. This sleepless, utterly narcotic state. I can scarcely believe any of it. I am still in the birth really. Not here yet. Oh, were there some time to recover.

I might have stayed there in that maternity wing forever. High up and safe. With all those women and babies and babies-to-be. In perfect white. Milky nights. The white waltzing across the polished floors. A prayer each morning over the PA system. If I could have stayed forever . . . Blood and milk and the life stuff of this universe—placenta, umbilicus, wish, desire, fear, beauty, brutality—all mixed together—tears, all that makes this human world. I'm not ready to go yet.

Manhattan completely rearranged after such an experience. I'm surprised it's there at all. From the maternity wing I could see from high up the avenues. God, it was beautiful.

Louis coming to visit in the hospital. Later I will learn he is afraid of hospitals and he is afraid of babies. He carries a little brass bell in the palm of his hand. *She is here!* A little panicked.

I must admit I am pretty shocked myself by her presence. As if she had been just dropped here in my lap out of the sky. As if I had not had those nine months at all. I suppose there was just no way to prepare.

The Moro reflex—which is a sort of gesture of astonishment in the hands, a kind of amazement in the baby, happening without the ability to control—first responses of the body. How very struck I am by the motion that so resembles a gesture at life's end I witnessed almost a year ago to the day—another spring. How much like darling Zenka who at the end of her life, seemingly asleep, would suddenly open her eyes with this same astonishment it seemed and flex her hands in just this way—so that her palms were up and her fingers outstretched. She was dying. Zenka, how I would have loved you to see this—despite your protestations—you always came around when it came to me. *I'm partial to you, my girl. You know that.* I loved you more than I can say. Here you are back in the startled motions of this new little one. We will go to Judith. We will visit your grave. I know you didn't think so, but with any luck I will see you again one day.

If I could scoop up that pale oval—which was your death, if I could—

And we float. Music of the spheres.

A cell of blood.
A white globule of milk.

Translucent amnion.
Perfection of the egg.
May we somehow stay safe.

Bodies moving through space, in a kind of flying, for a moment alight. Early fall, the stars aligned—to make this utter, utter perfection.

The baby cries without tears.

Emily cuts a piece of her baby blanket, which was once my sister's blanket, her mother's blanket, and gives it to baby Rose.

Everything seems elegiac. Emily and my mother in the kitchen making rose water. As if it is happening long ago in the past. They are both already long dead. I am watching their ghosts. And I? And Rose. We too are ghosts.

A flood of milk.

A bath of mother's milk.

At sanity's edge: drowning. Pull yourself together somehow, I think.

A great violence. The self being wrenched from the self. The part that broke away feeding on the other. No.

My breasts drowning the world—the baby in a cloud of white. Through her mother's milk she sees—what does she see?

Images appear and fall away. This strange place. The planet casts an eerie glare.

Walk with me into this light.

I look up at the diffuse moon—that heavenly body, full, spilling milk.

A pearl string of milk—I can see each tiny, tiny bead, on a string—between my breast and her mouth. And she sleeps.

The world a completely visceral, sensual place to her—heat and cold, light and shadow, darkness, sound. She does not know yet where my body ends and hers begins. Such utter helplessness. Such strange trust—at the mercy of this world. She breathes air now, she wears little clothes. She experiences pain—bellyaches. I did not ever want you to feel distress. It was nice I think for you inside. I'm sorry for the harshness. There are times when you seem inconsolable and I ask myself now, what have I done?

The burden of the love for this little creature. The responsibility I feel not only for her life, but for her death. That she will one day have to die. And it will be because of me.

To try to dispel some of the death I reach for the only salvation I know. An étude I was working on a while back. Want, for sanity's sake, to get out that piece about Elizabeth Bishop's love affair with a pregnant woman and then new mother to see how it strikes me.

23 JUNE

For perhaps the tenth time, the tenth time, the tenth time.

How was I to know that I was always just a shell? It keeps returning. How was I to know that I carried an emptiness so large, so wide inside me, like a child? Would the night devoid of stars realize it? Would the day without light? And that after those nine precious months I would become a shell again—only now to be so aware of it. How to know that the world would leave me this way forever—bereft.

> A nothing
> we were, are, shall
> remain flowering:
> the nothing—, the
> no one's rose . . .
>
> —*Paul Celan,* PSALM

A red mark called a stork's bite on the back of her neck.

The baby blissed out on milk. In a bliss of milk. She makes the most beautiful, satisfied face.

No sleep. If I dose for a moment—we are at my parents' house—and I wake to someone carrying the baby to me, I cannot believe it. It is like a dream, an enormous mistake of some sort. Whose baby is this, I wonder? Her little mouth already sucking as she nears me. What have I done?

The dark, the solitude, even with many people around, the quiet. Everything unreal and muffled. Too many people at once trying to take care of the baby. Too many phone calls. Work on our house still going on. The apartment too small—not an option. A trip to the city to see the pediatrician. I want to be left alone. I have never felt so strange and estranged. I weep all the time.

> Oh girl among the roses, oh crush of doves,
> oh fortress of fishes and rosebushes,
> your soul is a bottle filled with thirsty salt
> and your skin, a bell filled with grapes . . .
> Come to my heart dressed in white, with a bouquet
> of bloody roses and goblets of ashes,
> come with an apple and a horse,
> because there is a dark room there and a broken candle-
>   holder,
> and a dead dove, with a number.
>
> —*Pablo Neruda*

Is it day, is it night? Is it hot, is it cold? No knowing and time slips.

In the shock, in the fog.

Nothing is recognizable. Nothing familiar to me. Everything strange. Still there is music. And people I think I must, under different circumstances, love.

What have I done?

Mother.

This was meant to be a happy book.

The baby's ego disintegrates by the end of the day. Yes, I know the feeling.

The vertigo of being slammed back in an instant, not without violence, into one's small, singular life. The grace withdrawn. I mourn it more than I can describe.

Slammed back into yourself. Without preparation. You thought you were prepared. That perhaps was the hardest part.

The true violence of childbirth is the violence of being thrown back into your one mortal body—alone again. The strangeness of having only one body to live in.

No one is there. That much I am quite sure of.

The "I" despite my efforts at memoir here, despite my efforts of assertion, dissolves. The pregnancy was something to give me the impression that I exist. But it has been taken away. These traces on the page. The evidence of that sweet deception.

Babies respond to music almost immediately, I read. Most music falls between 50 and 150 beats per minute—the range of the human heart. And so it consoles. And shall always console.

How she reaches out onto open air—empty space

And how all the old feelings come streaming back—fear, sadness, dread. Only after nine months of respite, they seem magnified.

3 JULY

Killed a beast in the middle of the night for Rose's sake—a mosquito I think.

I have never killed anything in my life before.

The reaching toward a voice. The desperate attempt to locate, focus. I am grateful I do not remember being a baby. In many ways it seems a terrifying thing.

The days pass in a haze. One resembling the other—a little better, a little worse, that is all.

I pass her a perfect sphere of sleep, serenity, nourishment, pure health, and she passes the sleep back to me and we go on and on and on like this.

That mysterious milky globule.

Dissolving cell by cell by cell—a beautiful, irresolute music.

The eyes searching for the voice.

The hands searching. The look of yearning, want. I hold her to my heart. Try through tears to reassure her. But I cannot.

Rose, day twenty-four: nine pounds, thirteen ounces. Coco and Fauve are each seventeen pounds. Granted they are big.

Grow old with me, Helen, and I will support your head as you reach back into infancy. I want you to know this somehow—even though this is a period of terrible stress and hardship between us. And it seems right this minute as if I hate you. And I do. I do a little. Grow old.

Never leave my side.

Her tiny cup of unwept tears.

I give you this world.

Hymns to the Night.

A rose, asleep in the dark.

"And the ripe plum wears its dim attire." Keats, I think.

Oh, I am a lactating fool. Cannot, no matter what I do, stop crying.

The enzyme of sleep I pass to you through this milk. The enzyme of sleep you release in me.

A baby in July . . . blueberries in the mother's milk!

I am wearing a borrowed summer pregnancy/nursing frock. It is covered with flowers. I feel monstrous in this thing—five garish colors. But the baby stares and smiles and is utterly mesmerized by its patterns—it is clear she has never seen anything this beautiful. And so I put it on every day and cry.

I wonder why no one mentions how physically and emotionally depleting breast-feeding is. A very well-kept secret.

We pass the enzyme back and forth in something like peace.

Will you one day pass my immunities on to another generation? Long after I am gone.

The rose transfigured. The transfigured rose.

To have scarcely realized it—how very hard it would be—how impossible the world—how hard to stay alive without being able to write. A strange thing to say given the baby—and yet—how doomed I feel, how monstrously depressed. But given even a lucid half hour or so—a piece of paper—all is well—at least for the moment—at least that.

What kind of mother, I wonder, am I?

I catch the pacifier as it falls from her sleeping mouth—I guess I am that kind of mother in part.

I write this down while she cries—I guess I am that kind of mother too.

I can feel it already. The sort of mother I am going to be: violin lessons at three, alternative schools, Volvos, organic vegetables.

The sort who has waited her whole life, for her, for this. Who is going to do it right. Oh, God.

What, by the way, is a soccer mom?

16 JULY

One month old today. To mark how far one has come from that day of ultimate intensity—and to want it back perversely—*and not this.*

Now Elizabeth You Rest

The vast expanse of her Brazil becoming
improbable, flattened, abstracted
then finally blackening . . .

For perhaps the tenth time the tenth time the tenth time
today
and still I go under . . .

New Year's Eve—the length of beach lit up
Candles are burning in the sand—and—
Lilies released to the sea, floating, lilting
you looked to the sky . . .
A moon-lit night
Lota are you back in any guise?

For perhaps the tenth time the tenth time the tenth time . . .

Homeless once more you roam your child's
Nova Scotia
The mother now is put away
The mother now is put away again
And childish dreams and hopes are over gone and—
You wear your dim attire.

Now Elizabeth you rest your traveling head
If only for a moment there
A home. Something less than motion, restlessness

For a moment
Lilting, trembling world.
A home there on that globe

Orb lobe

The pregnant wife of a local painter.
26 years old.

You touch her cove and rest there
If only for a moment.
Nibble a swollen finger—all that grows, that lives
A flood of blood and world.
Rosy nipple
Lovely—low
Now lower—there
The glow.
Flow and lowing

Lowering toward
The glisten—linger.

Serene in that safe floating for a while like the child . . .
Sucking the pulse

As if a double heartbeat might . . .

Dispel and rest there—the prominence of the terrain
Your wandering, dreaming head—remembering
Lota.
She is dead by her own hand.
And her Brazil now *rain rainbow-ridden.*

Feign for a moment the vaguest hope,
Breathe. And catch your breath there.
Milky glow and wax and wane.

This staving off—small
Harbor, love brief
Respite child growing toward
Perfection.

She might fit inside a plum
She might fit inside a goose egg—
A pumpkin shell . . .

As if double heartbeats—the pregnant wife—
Then triple heartbeats might
Just might dispel if only for a moment then.

No coffee can wake you no coffee can wake you no coffee can wake you . . . You write but go no farther.

The traveler opens her daybook, but closes it again.
Opens it:
Days that cannot bring you near
or will not,
Distance trying to appear
something more than obstinate
argue, argue, argue with me.

Rest your roaming troubled head Elizabeth.
You're soaked in amber tilted lost a little
Caress and toss
And rest there
Something gives way a little
Those sweet coordinates
A lovely orb, a world
Alternately rose and rock and word.

This burning coast you lap at

And isn't it something like the map-maker's pinks
As you dip
Intensifying to rose—
Nova Scotia—snow on water
Flowers floating out, lit up

As you give in, lose a little
Gasp for breath and say good-bye now one more time those

Sweet high cries prefiguring
The yet to be born—
A lovely song in you
That cradles swaddles, protects you dear Elizabeth—
Homeless, grieving child.
And in that rosy bliss of milk and song, you rest.*

Disconcerting to say the least, to look down and see my face as a baby—my whole life about to begin.

Did my mother see a second chance in me?

Her sister used a pacifier until past the time she could go and buy them herself. Understandable, my mother said, not a very consoling childhood. Not a very comforting life. Did I bring this all back to her? Her first child. How could I have not?

17 JULY

How alien everyone and everything seems to me. Even Helen. Mom and Dad. The cats. The house. Everyone completely recognizable and yet utterly unfamiliar to me. How remote I feel. Far. They might be strangers. I do not feel at home here. It's like a particularly bad episode of the *Twilight Zone*. There seems no hope in the world. Such solitude. I walk into it, this black vortex, only this time cradling an infant.

---

*This is an étude about the poet Elizabeth Bishop, her long-term lover Lota who committed suicide, and Elizabeth's affair with a young pregnant woman.

Still I can write *black* and *vortex,* and that is always something.

The heroine contemplates suicide. Listening to *La Gianconda.*

> Wherever we turn in the storm of roses,
> the night is lit up by thorns, and the thunder
> of leaves, once so quiet within the bushes
> rumbling at our heels.
>
> —*Ingeborg Bachmann*

My hair comes out in fistfuls. I plant it in the sorrow garden. Late at night. So much silence.

John Cage: The music never stops. It is we who turn away.

Back at the Royal Pavilion at Brighton with Judith and Zenka and Christopher. It had rained on the journey down but cleared just as we arrived. After touring the mansion we walked far out on the boardwalk and were tossed by the Channel's fierce wind and waves. Judith and Zenka are both talking, but it's almost impossible to hear what they are saying. I am in the middle; they are holding my hands. It will be the last time we will all be together outside a hospital room. I can almost feel those waves today. Feel the wind on my face. And the tea and biscuits afterwards, having come in from the cold.

After the novels, after the teacups, after the skirts that trail across the floor—

Dear ones.

First dinner guests with the baby. Louis and Louise. Louis had just mowed the lawn and was a little cranky. Helen made a fish. Louise did an Omega dance.

Welcome to the world, Rose!
I am Rose my eyes are blue
I am Rose and who are you.
I am Rose and when I sing
I am Rose like anything.

Welcome to the world.

18 JULY

Rose sees her first rose, and is charmed—a yellow one—brought in from the garden.

My mother comes each week for two days—with a precious overnight in between. A time of great sweetness. Even if she is not entirely familiar to me. It's all right—no one is. It's a queer state I'm in. She brings us prepared food and is perfect with the baby and pampers me as much as she can while I basically feed the baby all day long and stare into empty space. Or on the odd day begin a perfectly unsuitable project like planting a huge new perennial garden. Plan to buy a thousand roses on sale in the fall. For Rose. A twenty-one-rose salute.

My mother is really the only one I trust with the baby. This includes myself.

Already, and it scarcely seems possible, Rose seems to connect the hand with the shadow the hand casts. My little pint-sized Plato in this our cave dwelling. Such isolation. Such small light.

20 JULY

Dreamt the baby disappeared in the night. I woke up screaming. The baby is in her bassinet, Helen says. So she is.

My internal chaos made manifest in our front yard. On the lawn: a NordicTrack, a Moses basket, a wok, a dumpster, a felt hat. It looks exactly like my interior world. Images out of surrealistic tableau—the world upside down. Thalia smiles. Each time she visits it's a little different. One experimental stage set after the next.

Well yes, according to Plato all learning is a kind of remembering of a world the soul saw before its birth, the vision of which it loses in the process of becoming embodied, but of which it can be reminded with carefully selected promptings. I believe this.

Bataille: We are discontinuous beings, individuals who perish in isolation in the midst of an incomprehensible adventure, but we yearn for our lost continuity. Our obsession is with a primal continuity linking us with everything that is.

How she has loved from the first day to be naked. And not curled in the fetal position. Her arms outstretched. A rose opening . . .

This little long-distance swimmer. Moving through the ocean of air. A July like no other.

Little marathon cyclist. Pedaling and pedaling in the dark. I remember another summer, La Tour de France. Ten years ago this month.

Little stepper, stepping and stepping. *Où vas tu?*

Barbara brings Rose her own Rose of Sharon tree! It is named Helene. We will plant it by the pond. Love it, watch it grow. Barbara is very, very fond of this little baby, I can tell.

Fran and the boys come to visit. She is most comforting, most kind. She says she wanted to kill Tobin in the beginning. Hated everyone and everything. She shows up now with her stories, just in the nick of time—remembering. Leslie Lawrence calls too. The most difficult of times. These wonderful mothers lending a hand. A genuine consolation.

Up all night every night. Each day spent doing interpretive dances with rabbit head and rattle. I am feeling very crazy.

It's only a very particular kind of day when I have the heart for certain things: giving the baby a real bath, trying a new breast-feeding position, using the baby sling. I need to do everything in my own tortoise time. Helen tries to force me and I snap at her, *I hate you, I hate you.* And I do. Everything at times overwhelming. Is it the lack of sleep? The blur of breast-feeding? The newness? Disorientation. Except for this notebook I haven't written a word. And what am I? Nothing I can recognize. It makes me very, very frightened.

The La Leche League people feel like a cult. *Don't even think of giving the baby a* bottle *of breast milk. She might not take it. You'll be out to dinner, you'll come home and she'll be screaming with hunger and then how will you feel?* They give me the creeps.

Disheartened to be the old self again. The cruel withdrawal of the happy hormones. Such well-being once. I'm sure of that.

It worries me now—but it is more true than almost anything else—that wherever I stood, there was always a part of me that was absent from the scene, apart. Something in me that was always elsewhere. And it was not that I was indifferent or passive, of which I was so often accused. Something was being held in reserve—and not entirely by choice.

Oh, literally thousands of things to worry about, now that I am my old self again.

When I look out my window a purple finch is feeding her babies in the eaves under the front porch.

Rose eats constantly today, it seems. Something about those birds.

When I can be objective and relaxed and at ease, which is almost never, I see she is a very, very sweet-tempered, charming little thing.

I happen to make excellent babies. We both agree.

When I take her outside I drape her body in my body's shadow. To shield her from the sun. As if one could.

Helen, when you say you will be home early I expect you to be here, because I am unraveling. More than usual.

The way the whole being searches for the voice—as if a figure out of Beckett. Yearns toward the voice.

The way the mouth searches for the thumb.

I seem to remember now my mother leaving a room or entering a room and how the world kept ending and beginning again. Darkness and then light. Shadows on the wall. Strange to be remembering such a thing now.

Shadows Roses Shadow

Under an alien sky
shadow roses
shadow
on an alien earth

between roses and shadows
in an alien water
my shadow
—*Ingeborg Bachmann*

How much solace still in poems.

That she has every sound and every syllable in every language ever known. And that after a year it shall disappear.

To be at once completely alert and completely helpless, lucid and bewildered. Not unlike the state I am in when writing. Difficult to articulate.

Ilene and I are both delighted to have each other to confide in about all this—the island of motherhood. I wish I could have been there for her five years ago when David was born. But I could not.

I did not rise above my flawed, mournful temperament. A sorrow to me still. Once we thought we might have a child together. Men never entered it. Clearly they were altogether far too high maintenance. Or that was my stance and I think I assumed it was hers. She is married now. To a very nice fellow indeed. He takes David on the back of his bicycle to Harlem for breakfast. They like to read the newspaper together.

A grave endeavor. It strikes me hard today. I have created something that is going to die.

Most miraculous being. Conceived in motion. Child of star and ocean and want. On a wing and a prayer. Child of deepest and most charmed, most precious and perfect night. The planets aligned. Diane comes to visit. She holds her like a charm. This sweet perfect little one. Forgive your mother, her doubts, her sorrow, all the weeping, rage, tears.

The two dwarf pear trees she planted in the field that were us. That is me, Helen, the one on the right, dying.

No need to mention the suicide notes composed in my head in the bleaker hours—or the little makeshift wills left here and there around the house. *In the event of my death . . .*

I wheel you around the peripheries of light—too bright—for now.

I will plant you a thousand roses.

The solitude doubles, then triples—as if I did not have enough to begin with.

Whenever I wonder what I am supposed to be doing, how to act, what to say, I ask myself—what would my mother have done? And then I do exactly that. It is a gift like no other in this world. All the judgment calls. All the sacrifices my mother made. The example of my mother's life.

You don't know how you got here—back to your impossibly warm bed—or where the other people went. It was a party maybe—voices, laughter, the clinking of glasses, all dissolved. Lulled to sleep in the back seat in what you knew was perfect safety and protection—washed and dressed in your pajamas and at home all of a sudden. When did that happen? All you know is that you're there—and that they saw to it. Without missing a beat. This perfect peace. My mother and father. That is the kind of parent I would like to be.

That the children should come first. My parents so unlike most parents, who were all so involved in their adultness or in their immaturity—trying to have a life, sure they were missing something, and they were, especially since they were all in their twenties back then. Of course they were missing a great deal.

But even at my age—I feel how much more I will have to forgo—my whole old way of life permanently altered. Already I can feel it. How much about giving up this will be. But I am well used to it. Another thing writing has taught me.

The silence is assertive, active these days. A third presence among us in the dark at night where the baby sucks and I pray.

The dizzying and terrifying shift seemingly overnight from no one can hurt us to no one can protect us.

And the old prayers come back automatically, involuntarily—without my consent exactly.

Lamb of God who takes away the sins of the world have mercy on us.

Lamb of God who takes away the sins of the world grant us peace.

I give you this world—Mozart, all kinds of music, poetry, mother's milk . . .

That I have created something so human, so vulnerable—this sensual being. Her obvious pleasure by the feeling of the air on her skin. Heat and light. Her desperate needs, wants—to be gratified.

Our time here is finite but for a little while. Placed in its crucible for nine months, it felt like a kind of infinity. Odd. Something to be savored. Not to be missed.

Nor the strangeness. The violence of birth. The beauty of creation. And all that serenity. And changing shape. And giving in. And sleep.

> Across mountains of heavenly floating roses
> From which one drops every night
> To reward the sleeper with the most beautiful dream
> of all.
>
> —*Robert Desnos*

My life more a mystery than ever.

Twinkle, twinkle, little star. How I wonder what you are.

And who can tell where one body ends and the other one starts. Or where the music begins, or where the music ends . . .

I love you. I think I can say that today.

Early evening. In another room she sleeps peacefully. I play with the baby monitor—the devise that listens in on her breathing, her sleep. I turn up the volume. Adjusting the silence.

Longing for that time again. Pregnancy—when it seemed time stopped or reversed itself. I grew younger and younger. My aging resumed again on the day of the baby's birth—or speeded up perhaps to compensate. This inexorable motion now. There'll be no going back. There will be no going back there again. To feel now as if I were being slammed into the future. A terrifying thing. But once, once for a precious, precious time—I was alive—*and I was not dying.*

Lamb inside. Our amniotic life. Through the rose window in my mind. It was a precious time.

And I am left with myself now. The baby already far off on a distant horizon, waving.

The baby twinkling. Dark star. Most perfect night.

Rocking on the rock-a-bye.

I shall never forget it—that florescence into which she was lifted.

They really do point with one tiny finger upward toward the heavens, like the infant Christ, in the great renaissance paintings.